The Agile Law Firm

Author
Chris Bull

Managing director
Sian O'Neill

The Agile Law Firm
is published by

Globe Law and Business Ltd
3 Mylor Close
Horsell
Woking
Surrey GU21 4DD
United Kingdom
Tel: +44 20 3745 4770
www.globelawandbusiness.com

Printed and bound in Great Britain by Ashford Colour Press Ltd

The Agile Law Firm

ISBN 9781787424548
EPUB ISBN 9781787424555
Adobe PDF ISBN 9781787424562
Mobi ISBN 9781787424579

© 2021 Globe Law and Business Ltd except where otherwise indicated.

The right of Chris Bull to be identified as the author of this work has been asserted by him in accordance with sections 77 and 78 of the Copyright, Designs and Patents Act 1988.

All rights reserved. No part of this publication may be reproduced in any material form (including photocopying, storing in any medium by electronic means or transmitting) without the written permission of the copyright owner, except in accordance with the provisions of the Copyright, Designs and Patents Act 1988 or under terms of a licence issued by the Copyright Licensing Agency Ltd, Shackleton House, Hay's Galleria, 4 Battle Bridge Lane, London, England, SE1 2HX, United Kingdom (www.cla.co.uk, email: licence@cla.co.uk). Applications for the copyright owner's written permission to reproduce any part of this publication should be addressed to the publisher.

DISCLAIMER
This publication is intended as a general guide only. The information and opinions which it contains are not intended to be a comprehensive study, or to provide legal or financial advice, and should not be treated as a substitute for legal advice concerning particular situations. Legal advice should always be sought before taking any action based on the information provided. The publishers bear no responsibility for any errors or omissions contained herein.

Table of contents

I. Welcome to the Agile world 5
  1. The Agile imperative 5
  2. The Agile organisation 7
  3. The Agile mindset 10
  4. How this Special Report works 11
  5. A word about you 13
  6. A brief history of Agile 15
  7. Ten attributes of the Agile organisation 21
  8. The limitations of Agile 23
  9. Introducing the Agile law firm 25

II. Client-centricity 33
  1. Clients at the centre 33
  2. Legal project management 41
  3. Legal project management today 44
  4. The role of the legal project manager 58
  5. Implementing LPM – should we apply LPM 59
     essentials to every client matter?
  6. Implementing LPM – how do we get our people 61
     engaged with LPM training?

III. Constantly innovating and improving 65
  1. Introducing innovation 65
  2. Lean and Six Sigma 77

IV.	**Insight-driven**	83
	1. Velocity	83
	2. The insight-driven firm	84
	3. Is data your 'new oil'?	87

V.	**Highly autonomous teams**	109
	1. Agile and the liquid workforce	109
	2. Designing the Agile network of teams	111
	3. Evolving teams into Agile teams	113

VI.	**The human dimension**	121
	1. Valuing individuals	121
	2. Becoming more human in the 2020s	123
	3. Rethinking our relationship with employees – adopting the EACH model	126
	4. The servant leader	130
	5. Agile performance management	131
	6. How Agile teams and project management enhance your human dimension	133

VII.	**Fluid and flexible (workplace and workforce)**	135
	1. The legal workplace and workforce reimagined	135
	2. Embracing Hybrid/Agile working	139

VIII.	**Organically collaborative**	149
	1. Network and platform organisations	149
	2. Collaborate to grow – the Agile growth strategy	151

IX.	**Restless, radical and challenging**	157
	1. Strategic agility	157
	2. The competitive imperative	165
	3. A new anatomy for your law firm – fit for the future	170
	4. Agile governance	173
	5. The next generation C-suite	176

X.	**Digital**	185
	1. Digital transformation	185
	2. The impact of technology on legal work	188

XI.	**United by a common purpose**	195
	1. Aligning with purpose	195
	2. Purpose into practice – being Agile about becoming Agile	196
	3. What now?	199

Notes	202
About the author	205
About Globe Law and Business	207

I. Welcome to the Agile world

1. The Agile imperative

Why wouldn't you want to be Agile? What is the alternative? The opposite to being Agile is being rigid, inflexible, immobile, slow, conservative, dogmatic. An organisation that's not Agile is bureaucratic, hierarchical, inward-looking and siloed.

Agility conjures up many different images. An Agile organisation will constantly anticipate, adjust, evolve, iterate, improve. It will respond to its clients and stakeholders with innovation, experimentation, anticipation and acceleration. Both clients and people within the firm describe it as organically fluid, flexible, dynamic and adaptive. It is egalitarian, diverse and inclusive.

If you work in a law firm today, which set of words best describe your firm? For a bonus point, would most of your clients and most of your people agree? If you do not work inside a law firm, you will have picked up this Special Report because you probably have some other involvement or interest in the legal world. Which set of words best describe what the term 'law firm' means to you? I wonder if there are some words and ideas in the previous paragraphs that felt like they simply did not belong in a description of law firms, or your specific firm.

Hold onto your response to that question. Maybe make a note of it. I suggest you come back to it, refining and reconsidering, as you dig deeper into the contents of this report, and I unwrap more of the elements that distinguish today's Agile organisations and the model for an Agile law firm. One thing I would like reading this report to prompt is a detailed answer to the question 'how Agile are we?'.

Throw 'Agile' into the title of just about any report today and you can claim to be plugging right into the zeitgeist. That's not because Agile is a newly minted concept. As the second part of this chapter will describe, many of the ideas that have coalesced into the Agile mindset and methodology have been around for decades. The Agile Manifesto, which really put the capital 'A' in Agile (and I will use that capital throughout when referring to Agile principles and methodologies) and triggered the sweeping adoption of Agile principles in the software industry is already 20 years' old. But Agile has kept building and attracting champions and advocates, hopping from sector to sector and working its way up the organisational ladder from shopfloor and developer's cubicle to boardroom. As the core principles of Agile have been adapted to form a new way of running entire organisations, they have obtained a new level of freshness, currency and timeliness for the 2020s.

"Crucial to the case for Agile, right here right now, is that it enables organisations to quickly adapt, embracing both ambiguity and constant change."

The economic, technological and societal trends of the 21st century have amplified the core messages of the Agile movement. You may be a little weary of hearing how we live in a VUCA world (volatile, uncertain, complex and ambiguous). I sympathise. But I am going to make that point again here and throughout this report, which is also about the external forces and rapidly changing conditions that are reshaping the legal universe. Crucial to the case for Agile, right here right now, is that it enables organisations to quickly adapt, embracing both ambiguity and constant change. That last sentence is another one to consider for a minute in relation to your firm today. It isn't a description I would apply to many of the law firms I have met and worked with. In recent years, though, I have cheered on the growing numbers of individuals and sometimes entire teams in firms who have begun to aspire to it and influence their colleagues.

The electric jolt of COVID-19 in 2020 underlined the volatility and unpredictability of our world, setting off a chain reaction of changes in our lives and businesses that we are still processing. Agile became one of the most used words of that year. Individuals and organisations had to adapt at speed to very different conditions following the outbreak of COVID-19 and, in many ways, the response demonstrated just how adaptive we have already become. More specifically, new ways of working were adopted almost instantly in response to lockdown and isolation. Those huge changes to our work locations, schedules, communications and infrastructure impacted the legal sector dramatically as well; suddenly, most of us were Agile workers. We did not, however, find ourselves all suddenly working in Agile organisations. But 2020 demonstrated very vividly just why being an Agile and adaptive organisation, one which automatically adjusts its process and performance to current conditions, was going to be so critical for our future. UK-based legal tech and innovation guru Derek Southall, of Hyperscale Group, asks us to "question whether the BC ('Before COVID-19') structures and processes are fit for a more complex PC ('Post COVID-19') world?"[1]

Agility is the capacity of an organisation to adapt to new conditions and to change its direction. This capacity is enshrined in a critical Agile concept, the pivot, which was the US Association of National Advertisers' *Word of the Year* for 2020,[2] and which I will return to later in the report. The dictionary definition of agility is 'nimbleness'. That quality is the opposite of rigidity, inertia and passivity. Firms marked by complacency, endemic risk aversion and an inability to respond quickly and easily are a long way from Agile.

2. The Agile organisation
Organisations which identify themselves as Agile are not simply moving faster or responding more quickly. At the heart of genuine

organisational agility are an interesting, apparently paradoxical, pair of fundamental values – Agile organisations are both more *human* and more *digital* than the rest. The interplay between those two principles is central to the proposition that law firms can, indeed should, be Agile organisations.

Only over the last decade has Agile begun to offer a more serious and comprehensive answer to the bigger question of how successful businesses can operate in a 21st-century model, when bureaucracy doesn't work as the default operating system. Traditional models of management and corporate governance have been failing to keep up with the demands of the modern economy and new approaches were urgently needed. As leading Agile thinker and author of *The Age of Agile*, Steven Denning, puts it: "In some ways, the new way of running an organization is still the best-kept management secret on the planet".[3]

The roll call of organisations that identify themselves, and are regularly cited, as Agile champions is an impressive list of the outstanding business success stories of the century. They include Netflix, Amazon, Spotify, Salesforce, Gore, Google, Patagonia, Whole Foods, Tencent, Pixar, Starbucks, Airbnb and Chinese white-goods giant Haier. Longer-standing global companies that have embraced major Agile programmes include Ericsson, Barclays, Fidelity Investments and Microsoft. These companies have taken the Agile blueprint and evolved it into an entire alternative ecosystem.

There are even more case studies of successful entrepreneurial and start-up Agile models. It is widely acknowledged that it is easier to set up Agile in the first place than to transition from a conventional, 20th-century way of working. It is also simpler to implement Agile across a smaller organisation. Indeed, I predict that adopting the Agile model for small and start-up legal businesses of all kinds will become not just relatively simple but replace the alternative command and control default long before the 2020s are over. Given that trend, this report presents not some kind of fringe alternative model for running a firm, but outlines the most likely blueprint for modern firm organisation. Don't forget – the future is always born out on the fringes.

I would not have been invited to write this Special Report if the embrace of Agile was still something restricted to industries like software, manufacturing and consumer tech. If, like many new business ideas, Agile, while sweeping across corporate boardrooms and shopfloors, was having no impact on the world of legal and professional services, this report would probably be premature. As I will show, however, the anatomy of the modern law firm is itself

"It is widely acknowledged that it is easier to set up Agile in the first place than to transition from a conventional, 20th-century way of working. It is also simpler to implement Agile across a smaller organisation."

being redesigned and reinvented at a rapid pace and the direction of that change embodies many of the key principles of Agile. At a practical level, progressive legal organisations of all kinds have been using many of the new methods and tools that I refer to in this report as the Agile toolkit. These change projects are generating big leaps forward in how legal matters or projects are managed, client service and experience is designed and tech-enabled legal products are developed.

Just a look at the titles of some of the best writing on the 21st-century law firm – all recommended reading – immediately conveys the message that we have arrived at a tipping-point that marks the end of one era and beginning of another in the evolution of law firms: Jordan Furlong, *Law is a Buyer's Market*[4]; George Beaton and Imme Kaschner, *Remaking Law Firms*[5]; Jack Newton, *The Client-Centered Law Firm*[6]; Heidi Gardner, *Smart Collaboration*[7]; Michele DeStefano and Guenther Dobrauz-Saldapenna (eds), *New Suits*[8]; and, dealing with the broader background, the works of Professor Richard Susskind and Daniel Susskind including *The End of Lawyers?*[9]; *The Future of the Professions*[10]; and *A World Without Work*.[11] This body of thought about the state and future of the legal industry, and many other books and articles on the same theme, unite around a common central view that our law firm world is transforming at an ever-accelerating pace. And these works were all written pre-2020 and COVID-19.

Today, I describe legal services as an industry trying to cram 20 or 30 years of deferred evolution into just a few years, now having to run even faster pursued by a virus, widespread virtualisation and economic disruption. My stance on whether law firms are ready to become truly Agile is 'opto-pessimist'. That is not just fence-sitting! There are some strong pillars of the law firm model and mindset that, contrary to popular opinion, make them a natural fit for an Agile approach. I will describe some of these in the final part of this chapter. Conversely, I worry that law firms are too unquestioning of the most rigid, hierarchical and outdated aspects of their set-up – big obstacles on any Agile journey. The COVID-19 crisis has changed the way law firms work forever, but the economic impact on them has, overall and so far, been limited and so the understandable complacency of financially thriving firms dampens the appetite for change.

3. The Agile mindset

Agile is a mindset. I will return later to the ultimate futility of trying to introduce or impose Agile tools, methodologies and processes without that genuine commitment to its principles. If you want to reap the benefits of becoming a truly Agile firm you will need to transform the vestiges of old, unadaptive, hierarchical management into a new client-engaged, team-empowered model.

"If you want to reap the benefits of becoming a truly Agile firm you will need to transform the vestiges of old, unadaptive, hierarchical management into a new client-engaged, team-empowered model."

Adopting the mindset is essential. That will not always be easy for law firms, as I will explain. Setting out on the journey to become Agile will represent a culture change for the majority of firms. A firm will not become Agile overnight, something we can learn from the big Agile champions of the corporate world whose progress has been carved out over a number of years.

However, shifting your mindset and accepting a new idea does not, by itself, equal business success. Embracing the Agile client value mindset must be followed up with action. For most law firms that means transforming strategy, behaviours, systems, processes, structures, metrics, rewards, language and attitudes. That is why there is a store-cupboard of tools and practical, implementable ideas to support the Agile journey. That is where most of this report will focus.

The word Agile appears a lot in these pages. It is a widely used term in management, technology and societal thinking these days and the term is applied to a lot of different methods and tools, many of which I will introduce and explain. There are also plenty of influential ideas that I will cover that are closely associated and aligned with the basic principles of Agile, even if they don't have the Agile label. I am not an Agile purist and one aim of this report is to show how these ideas can grow into a bigger, overarching programme. So, I feature influential ideas such as Lean, design thinking and legal project management and explain how they support and fit with the overall Agile law firm. I don't expect law firms to get preoccupied with what things are called. What is important is that firms engage with this new, intrinsically 21st-century management philosophy that is gaining ground and adherents across the world.

This report synthesises and explores a lot of big ideas. It explains how this Agile movement can be harnessed by law firms. Gary Hamel is ranked as the world's most influential business thinker by *The Wall Street Journal*. His iconoclastic work as a consultant and as Director of the Management Lab at London Business School is focused on reinventing management and building organisations that are "fit for the future". My hope is that the next few years will see a growing number of law firms become what Hamel describes as "post-bureaucratic organizations" – a synonym for Agile – embodying "the ground-breaking ideas and practices that are remaking the foundations of human organization ... building an organization that can thrive in a world of unrelenting change".[12]

4. How this Special Report works
Producing this Special Report seemed like a more straightforward proposition when I accepted Globe's invitation to write it. That was back in what now feels like a different world, before we had heard of

COVID-19. It was also before I realised that what was required for the legal market was not just another 'how to' guide to deploying specific Agile tools and techniques. What I have ended up trying to produce is a consolidated, broader and more strategic guide to the emerging business blueprint of the 21st century – the Agile organisation – and a practical exploration of what the Agile law firm looks like. This report is a manifesto, a manual and a map.

In the remainder of this chapter I will finish building the foundations for that guide. Too often, as consultants and advisers, we can be guilty of leaping in without providing the essential background on just where ideas have come from, how they have been used and developed and why they are important. This chapter closes with sections covering a brief history of Agile, an introduction to the 10 Agile Attributes and my take on why Agile is so important for today's law firms.

As the core of this report, I explore each of the 10 Attributes of an Agile firm in some detail. The report takes readers on a journey through those dimensions, building up a picture of the interlocking components that characterise an Agile organisation. These are the main sections of the report and the 10 chapters are organised into themes: *people and teams*; *clients and service*; *strategy and organisation*. I have attempted to summarise not just the principles and background to each Agile Attribute, but also give practical advice on getting started and on using specific tools and methods in that area of your firm. In each section, I provide readers with some ideas about what to do next – how can you improve your firm's agility and where do you start. And things you should probably stop. Because, in the words of the hugely influential management thinker, Peter Drucker, "If you want something new, you have to stop doing something old".[13]

Throughout this report there are recurring features to help readers use the material in their own organisation:

- *Agile first steps* – a short set of suggested actions for firms wanting to get started on their Agile journey. They also function as a quick-fire litmus test of *'how Agile is your firm?'*. If your honest and objective response to the recommendations is that many are already underway, or are even fully completed, you are already on your Agile journey. Not every step will suit every firm and that suitability will depend on your current level of agility, size, type of work, business model and culture. Nor is this an exhaustive summary of every idea, recommendation or tool contained in the chapter – if you only read the 'first steps' I promise you will be missing a lot of other great stuff! And, finally, I'd advise you not to try to take every step all at once – I have been a bit over-generous in these sections and perhaps 'first,

second and third steps' might have been more precisely accurate.
- *Agile toolkit* sections feature throughout the report and make up a substantial proportion of the content. In these, I take a deeper dive into the main Agile methodologies or tools. Most of these originated in business environments a long way from law firms but have been adapted and developed over the last decade or so and used in multiple legal settings. If you want to learn more about the following tools and how they might work – or work better – in your firm, then this report is designed to give you a quick introduction and some ideas for getting started. The Agile toolkit includes:
  - Agile and Scrum product development and project management;
  - legal project management (LPM);
  - Kanban;
  - Lean;
  - Six Sigma;
  - design thinking;
  - insight driven organisations (IDO) and the information/insight/impact model;
  - 'jobs to be done' theory; and
  - Hybrid/Agile working.

5. A word about you

Like most authors I can only guess the identities and roles of the people who will read this report. It seems likely that a good proportion of the readership will be made up of those who currently work in legal service firms, thanks to the title and the Globe Law and Business audience. If that describes you, whether you are a managing/senior partner or chief executive, client-facing partner or lawyer, senior manager or someone working in another role but interested in the management and improvement of law firms, then you should find a lot of the report aimed squarely at you. Where I talk about law firms I am, of necessity, having to cover a huge spectrum of organisations of very different shapes and sizes, with different headcount and turnover numbers. I think you will find that the way I describe suggestions for review and action is pitched broadly at the mid-tier of law firms; firms with 100+ people, multiple partners/owners and probably multiple locations. However, where I think it is helpful, I have made some specific comments to help sole traders and very small firms or, in some cases, directly addressed the largest 'Big Law' firms.

As one look at my biography will tell you, I have spent more time than most legal consultants and business thinkers working with 'alternative legal service provider' (ALSP) players, in addition to my years inside law firms and all four of the Big 4 accounting firms. I am, therefore,

"I do think, however, that many of the more recently established providers referred to as 'newlaw', ALSP or law company tend to have begun, day one, with a more Agile model than conventional law firm partnerships."

acutely conscious that those ALSPs do not, in the main, refer to themselves as *law firms* and might consider being bundled into that category alongside traditional firms as some kind of an affront. I do not think an apology is in order, however. I am using law firm as a neat shorthand here for legal service provider. *Law firm* for the purposes of this report could be a partnership or a company, a business with hundreds of years' pedigree or a new start-up. I do think, however, that many of the more recently established providers referred to as 'newlaw', ALSP or law company tend to have begun, day one, with a more Agile model than conventional law firm partnerships.

I use the terms 'you' and 'your firm' in this report, particularly when I am suggesting questions or actions you should consider. For readers who are not working in a law firm or legal service business of any kind today, apologies. If you work with the legal sector as a consultant, technology or service provider or have worked in law firms in the past, I suggest you have one, or more, law firm you know in mind as you read. That will allow you to engage with the questions, including *how Agile are you?*, and I think you will get something extra out of the report. If you work client-side, in a corporate legal function or similar, then, welcome! I am delighted that law firm clients have picked up this report, which emphasises constantly that the transition to become an Agile law firm is, first and foremost, a shift to be more client-centric.

You may, like other readers who are not working inside a law firm, be able to answer some of the questions in the core chapters by reference to a law firm you know or work with closely. Indeed, that might be an enlightening, possibly entertaining, activity!

6. A brief history of Agile

Agile with a capital 'A' began life as an approach to software development in the 1990s. It was a response to shortcomings with the traditional highly planned and sequential approach known as 'Waterfall', which was focused on extensive documents, long planning cycles and strict control. Too many Waterfall projects proved hard to adjust or adapt and often took a long time to deliver anything. Different business functions did not commonly work together but were separated and worked through sequentially. These limitations were more exposed as user and customer expectations changed more regularly and as technology advances accelerated. Simple, intuitive, and responsive became the watchwords for great software. Agile methodology instead focuses on short steps, embracing and adapting to continuous change, and small, frequent releases that emphasise customer value.

The foundational document of the movement is the 2001 Manifesto for Software Development – now commonly called the *Agile Manifesto*. The Manifesto emerged from the software industry back in 2001, forged at a meeting of enthusiasts in Snowbird, Utah. It specified the four articles (or values) and 12 principles that have come to define Agile. Where the Waterfall approach mandates lots of up-front design and planning and tries to capture all requirements as early as possible, the Agile approach instead assumes that not all requirements can be known before work is begun.

The four articles in the Agile Manifesto (Agile Alliance, 2001)[14] are founded in the world of software development but are pitched at a much more universal level than that, sowing the seeds for the broader application of Agile to running organisations that is the focus of this report. They are[15]:

Article One. We value individuals and interactions over processes and tools.

Article Two. We value working software over comprehensive documentation.

Article Three. We value customer collaboration over contract negotiations.

Article Four. We value responding to change over following a plan.

Supporting the Agile Manifesto are 12 Agile principles. The majority are good project management practices that had been in use for many years. Agile, however, refined and connected these principles into a new working approach.

> **The Agile principles**[16]
> - Satisfy the customer through early and continuous delivery of valuable service/software.
> - Welcome change even late in development. Agile is a change-driven approach – *we should not simply expect change, but welcome it.*
> - Deliver software frequently from a couple of weeks to a couple of months, with a preference for the shorter timescale – breaking large deliverables into smaller, more manageable pieces.
> - Business people and developers must work together daily throughout the project.
> - Build projects around motivated individuals.
> - The most efficient and effective method of conveying information to and within a development team is face-to-face conversation.
> - Working product or service is the primary measure of progress – the quality of the end result is the key metric.
> - Agile processes promote sustainable development – Agile project teams that have some history of working together can calculate their productivity rate, or velocity.
> - Continuous attention to technical excellence and good design enhances agility.
> - Simplicity – the art of maximising the work not done – is essential.
> - The best requirements and designs emerge from self-organising teams.
> - At regular intervals, the team reflects on how to become more effective, and then fine-tunes and adjusts.

In due course, the Agile Manifesto spawned supporting methodologies including Scrum, DevOps and Kanban. All of these are variations of Agile thinking. In some organisations they have developed to become the sole variant in use and the emphasis is on that methodology – you will often hear of organisations that have deployed 'DevOps' or 'Scrum' rather than Agile. In others, Agile is the standard around which an initiative is centred and it is backed up by cherry-picking from the other detailed tools and techniques. There are now more than 40 labels that are used for the various flavours of Agile.

Agile thinking and methodologies were not suddenly 'invented' in 2001, however, nor are they by any means solely the creation of the

US software industry. The Agile Manifesto and subsequent development of multiple variants draws on a long history of continuous improvement ideas.

In particular, the role of the Toyota production model and Lean methodologies in the development of Agile is crucial. In the middle of the 20th century, Taiichi Ohno and others at Toyota identified that small demand-driven iterations generally turned out to be more efficient than mass-production runs. By emphasising 'flow' through the production system and ruthlessly eliminating waste the manufacturing process could be radically transformed and improved. Toyota's system itself was a reworking and enhancement of thinking developed in the motor industry by Ford, decades earlier.

In 1990, the Toyota iterative small-team approach found a much wider audience as a result of the description of "lean manufacturing" – or just *Lean* – in the classic book *The Machine That Changed the World*[17] based on the Massachusetts Institute of Technology $5 million five-year study on the future of the automobile. Management thinkers and manufacturing executives built on the production system, developed the idea of a broader 'quality system' and synthesised its principles with other ideas over the following two decades.

Following the launch of the Agile Manifesto in 2001, there was a flurry of innovative thinking fusing those Agile principles with Lean. In 2003, a now classic book on software development, *Lean Software Development: An Agile Toolkit*[18] translated the lean manufacturing principles of the Toyota Production System to the software development and services domain. Lean and Agile principles began to be commonly combined and a whole series of new spin-offs took these core ideas into an ever-wider constellation of sectors, moving way beyond manufacturing and software into retail, financial services, government and even into law.

Scrum is probably the principal Agile methodology in use. It uses a cross-functional team-based approach for delivering value to customers, with specific defined roles such as product owner and Scrum master. The key components of Scrum are often referred to as Agile and vice versa. An Agile project at small Czech law firm Holubova Advokati,[19] advised by consultants from Agile Lawyer, deployed the Scrum methodology, with roles like product owner and Scrum master translated from the technology to the legal industry. However, it is fair to say that the full Scrum toolkit was developed specifically for software development and requires a lot of adaptation to legal work.

Kanban ('visible record' in Japanese) is derived from both traditional and more modern Japanese concepts and was another innovation originally spawned by Toyota as part of their production system. Kanban cards carried critical data backwards and forwards through the manufacturing process allowing flow and waste to be more effectively measured. As part of the rapid evolution of Agile in the 2000s, Kanban was enlisted to support Scrum projects and developed into the concept of *Kanban boards*, that would provide essential information about the workload and state of play for an Agile team in a highly effective and visual way. Since 2009, Kanban has been developed and tailored for a whole series of industries and proven to be a very popular, relatively simple way of introducing Agile and Lean principles into real-life work management. The use of Kanban in legal will show up again later in this report.

Lean Startup is a methodology for developing businesses and products based on the hypothesis that if new firms invest time into deeply exploring the needs of customers, they can reduce risk, reduce the need for initial funding, and enhance the chance of ultimate success. This builds on Agile principles and other management and product development ideas, including Lean, design thinking and customer development. The concept of continuous learning, which I will return to later, is central to Lean Startup, which was popularised by Erie Ries's 2011 book.[20]

Design thinking is a human-centred approach to innovation that seeks to integrate the needs of people, the possibilities of technology, and the requirements for business success. Design thinking was further adapted for business purposes by the design consultancy IDEO.[21]

McKinsey have done more to advance the evolution of Agile management thinking than most. Their research and a string of articles in the first half of the 2010s evolved into the 'Agile Tribe', a group of over 50 global consultants with expertise from digital, operations, marketing and organisation design. A good example of McKinsey Tribe thinking and research is their January 2018 article "The Five Trademarks of Agile Organisations".[22] When asked in a 2017 McKinsey survey[23] where companies apply Agile ways of working, respondents most often identified activities that are naturally closest to the customer: innovation, customer experience, sales and servicing and product management. This is not too surprising, since customer-centricity is cited most often – followed by productivity and employee engagement – as the objective of Agile transformations.

In 2016, Darrell K Rigby, Jeff Sutherland and Hirotaka Takeuchi in their article "Embracing Agile", proclaimed the advent of Agile as a broader, more strategic management idea.[24] That heralded the next phase of Agile development as Agile management methodologies, offering a radical alternative to command and control-style management, began to influence a broader range of industries up to and including the C-suite. Two years later, Agile was a *Harvard Business Review* cover story[25] and a bona fide business management trend, fuelled by the continued growth of the world's largest companies and a fascination with the part Agile plays in their success.

Steven Denning reported back from the 2019 Drucker Forum Conference,[26] one of the biggest annual global business management events, on the consensus view that a new approach to management and innovation was taking hold across the business world. He highlighted the shifts from an overwhelming focus on financial targets, specifically the idea of maximising shareholder value, towards creating more value for customers; from a primarily vertical and hierarchical to a horizontal and collaborative ecosystem; and from top-down bureaucracy to small autonomous teams. That wave of new thinking is, nevertheless, still emerging and not yet either dominant or universal.

While business thinkers and consultants consistently proclaiming the dawn of a new way of managing organisations is important, the more compelling evidence has to be the dramatic 21st-century business success of organisations who have Agile at their core. As noted earlier, Agile companies include many of the most valuable and innovative

"Customer-centricity is cited most often – followed by productivity and employee engagement – as the objective of Agile transformations."

businesses of the century including Netflix, Amazon, Spotify, Google, Tencent, Pixar, Airbnb, Facebook and Microsoft. These companies operate on rapid cycles of evaluation, decision, iteration and implementation, with most of this activity taking place in self-managed teams that sit close to the client, rather than at the 'top' or 'centre'.

The Agile model has been expanded out by many of these pioneers and evolved into the Platform or Ecosystem organisation. This model is that of a network, with every employee having agency and autonomy and collaborating in a fluid, shifting ecosystem with their colleagues, as well as other organisations and customers. When you see constant references to 'platform models', which can now be spotted in the legal world, they are rooted in this much less rigid and boundaried concept of modern organisations. The now ubiquitous, but still very recent, concept of the App Store, with myriad different companies and often individuals all collaborating and connected via that platform is often used to explain the direction of travel for Agile organisations. Steven Denning describes this shift of focus, in every industry, as being from *hardware* to *software* – replacing the rigid, rooted dimensions of your client offering (the 'hardware') with the responsive, customisable and constantly improving elements (the 'software').[27]

"The prevalent organisational model for the most successful businesses in our VUCA world is Agile. Now is the time for law firms to take that lesson and adopt their own model for the new decade."

Most Agile organisations are built largely from intangibles – knowledge, brand, expertise, processes, collaborative networks, service excellence, though to some extent these are packaged up into more tangible building blocks like applications and products. That represents a fundamental divide from the old economy champions built on tangible assets. This is an evolution that is just as relevant to law firms. The old model law firm is a construct of tangible human assets – fundamentally lawyers and their time. The new Agile law firm foregrounds intangibles like knowledge, brand, expertise and the collaborative network.

Before I summarise the key attributes of the Agile organisation, there is an important point to make about the companies listed above. It is undoubtedly a hall of fame of many of the most spectacular business successes of the last 20 years. They have all deployed Agile methodologies and are recognised as standard-bearers for this new management paradigm. Most of these companies are 'digital natives'. We might *expect* them to adopt a different model from the established market leaders who grew and matured before the Millennium and global financial crisis of 2008/09. But the correlation between their business success and their Agile model is critical. These well-known models are founded on obsessing about customer experience, both anticipating and responding to customer needs. They excel at tracking and leveraging – and sometimes creating – the latest technological breakthroughs and empowering small teams to constantly innovate. The prevalent organisational model for the most successful businesses in our VUCA world is Agile. Now is the time for law firms to take that lesson and adopt their own model for the new decade.

7. Ten attributes of the Agile organisation

I am not going to pretend that there is a single, undisputed and neatly wrapped definition of an Agile organisation. The relatively recent application of Agile concepts to a whole entity and the continued evolution of those concepts in new directions mean that these ideas are still in flux. But, in this section, I will introduce you to my 10 Agile Attributes that form the basis of the following chapters and represent the most commonly cited capabilities of an Agile organisation. These are, effectively, how we differentiate the emerging 21st-century Agile management model from the declining 20th-century organisational bureaucracy.

Any organisation-wide Agile transformation needs to have a big impact in lots of places: client experience, strategy, structure, people, process and technology. Presenting a list of 10 Agile Attributes with a chapter on each might suggest they stand alone. In fact, the attributes overlap and interlock, but it is important to bring some structure to the content and to highlight the most important dimensions of any Agile journey. The Agile Attributes are organised into three groups: clients and service; people and teams; strategy and organisation.

> **The 10 Agile Attributes**
>
> Clients and service
> *Client-centric* – place the customer/client experience at the centre of everything you do and obsessively looking at every challenge, change and decision from the customer's perspective. Defining and measuring performance in terms of customer/client value.
>
> *Constantly innovating and improving* – embed rapid cycles of client-focused design and improvement throughout the firm. Deploy agile tools like sprints, Kanban and design thinking. The entire organisation is orientated to innovate and intently focused on continuously looking to optimise quality.
>
> *Insight-driven* – converts information into insight into business impact, rapidly responding to and anticipating changes in their customer base, market, technology and society. Faster decision making, learning, time to market and reconfiguration than most organisations.
>
> People and teams
> *Built around highly autonomous teams* – teams, ideally multi-disciplinary and close to the customer, are empowered to make critical business decisions rapidly and without bureaucratic interference.
>
> *Human* – everyone working in an Agile organisation is empowered and engaged, with a high sense of responsibility and agency. People are treated as both adults and customers.
>
> *Fluid and flexible (workplace and workforce)* – the people model is flexed in response to changes and demands. Rigid elements are loosened or eliminated, resulting in a highly inclusive and diverse population capable of working from anywhere, with full-time, part-time, permanent, contracted-out and flex resources.
>
> *Organically collaborative* – skills, knowledge, ideas and expertise from anywhere across the organisation – and beyond it – are naturally pulled together in order to maximise customer value. Organisational barriers and disincentives to collaboration are dismantled. The organisation is a connected network of teams.

> **Strategy and organisation**
> *Restless, radical and challenging* – do not accept received wisdom, assumptions or models developed in very different times without challenge or review. Innovate in every part of the organisation, from business model to customer service to remuneration and recognition. Think the unthinkable!
>
> *Digital* – smart deployment of leading-edge technologies allowing the Agile organisation to meet changing customer needs, liberate its teams and people and innovate more.
>
> *United by a common purpose* – autonomous and empowered teams only work in purpose-led organisations with a strong and clearly defined ambition that enthusiastically engages its people. That ambition should be clearly stated and universally understood.

8. The limitations of Agile

Full-organisation agility is still maturing and gaining adherents. Even so, there are already poster-child big corporations who are Agile champions, as we have seen. While tech sector leaders have pioneered Agile working, the list of champions extends beyond just the one sector and includes plenty of leading companies from other industries, including Tesla, Whole Foods, Patagonia, Gore and Barclays.

There are, however, some real pitfalls to avoid and lessons to learn if you are trying to scale your compact Agile outfit into a major, mature Agile organisation or to adopt Agile in what has been, thus far, a traditional environment. In fact, most of the businesses seen as Agile pioneers experienced major setbacks in the early days. The idea of arriving at some final Agile 'destination' with journey completed, after which you can take your foot off the improvement and innovation pedal is, in today's world, a nonsense. If the world keeps spinning, and change in technology, society and the economy keeps accelerating, organisations need to respond and evolve – 2020 drove that point home. Possibly one of the hardest pills for lawyers to swallow if they do make a shift to an Agile model is that it will, inevitably, always be evolving.

Becoming more Agile is an imperative. But adopting the basic building blocks of Agile may deliver limited impact if there are restrictions elsewhere in the firm's management, governance or if there are conflicting processes. While those restrictions are usually the legacy of the firm's old operating model, there are also some specific situations where Agile methodologies may not have the same scale of benefits as elsewhere. One example is if your work is very heavily regulated and bound by strict compliance rules that give minimal latitude to find new and better ways of doing things. That can make processes and client

"This is one of the biggest challenges in going Agile – expanding it out to an entire organisation, beyond a handful of early-adopter teams or one function, radically challenges foundational structures and cultures."

service relatively impervious to Agile improvements. Similarly, if there is little opportunity for client feedback, one of the primary sources of Agile innovation is removed. Finally, if there is limited scope for improvement – certainly in the short term – where work tasks are either so simple and routine or already so efficiently performed or so quick and easy to change that there is almost no waste or failure. What I will stress at this point is that I do not believe that the majority of legal workflows fall fully into any of these categories. Certainly, there are areas of legal practice that are run on a rigid set of government or regulatory guidelines and other areas which have become simpler, more commoditised and efficient over the last two decades. However, these are the exceptions and not the rule and within them there remains scope for applying the kind of detailed Agile tools that the following chapters describe.

In surveys done by Steven Denning's SD Learning Consortium, 80–90% of Agile teams acknowledged tensions between their local Agile practices and those of the overall company.[28] This is one of the biggest challenges in going Agile – expanding it out to an entire organisation, beyond a handful of early-adopter teams or one function, radically challenges foundational structures and cultures.

I hear two interesting arguments when people initially push-back against Agile programmes, admittedly alongside a lot of more conventional resistance to change and 'not in my backyard' behaviour. In both cases these objections challenge whether the Agile journey we are embarking on will in fact end up restricting freedom of movement and autonomy, rather than expanding it. I hear the complaint that this 'so-called Agile' world seems to have a lot of rules, processes and methodologies. There is some truth in this. To become an Agile firm you will need to deploy at least some of the approaches in the toolkit. Like all approaches that have been developed to improve working practices and honed over time, they come with rules, guidance and a new language. Deploying them will certainly add some more rigour to the way projects and processes are tackled. In law firms this may be adding additional structure into tasks that, if they have been performed at all, have been considered as non-billable. That can be a tough sell. The case for Agile here is that you will create new value through client-centred innovation and improvement that you simply were not getting to without the structure of the Agile tools. Additionally, these new routines, once your teams are used to them, should operate quickly and efficiently – an important facet of Agile.

The second interesting concern raised is that the intense emphasis on discovering the genuine needs, experiences and perceptions of clients is too time-consuming. Lawyers, particularly senior ones, can object to the apparent disregard of their own years of experience and finely honed 'gut feel' instinct. "I know my client very well, thank you" is a well-used phrase. There is a strong, cultural inclination, hardly unique to lawyers, to jump in with a solution right away and rely on assumptions instead of actually listening to clients which is ironic given that legal training emphasises the exact opposite.

9. Introducing the Agile law firm
The COVID-19 pandemic was such a powerful disruptive event that it effectively reset the counter on organisational change across all sectors, including law. I believe the era of the Agile law firm will begin, finally, in 2021. Many of the firms I have spoken to in depth, including for this report, are keen to point out how much change and progress there has been in recent years in their firms. Many firms were in a much better position to respond in March 2020 when lockdowns began to hit home than they would have been only six months before. They benefited from the compound impact of mobile technology roll-outs, an accelerated shift to cloud computing, more agile and flexible working practices and the early experiments with Agile in the years running up to 2020. However, none of those firms deny that spring 2020 represented a watershed moment, after which things would never be the same again. One law firm leader I interviewed described it as seeing "the certainties blown away". Another echoed one of the most common reflections on what changed in law firms in 2020: "our

people's perception and engagement with technology and innovation has changed almost overnight, and for good".

Plenty of observers, way smarter than I, have predicted, observed and analysed the slow decline of the traditional law firm model. Yet even under intense pressure during 2008/09 and 2020, it has seemed to be surprisingly, defiantly resilient. All the time, under the skin, it has been shifting and adapting, transitioning slowly and often very subtly, continuously nudged in a new direction by external forces.

But what is the new model, or – more likely – the multiple new models, that will replace it? That is what this report is about. I have pulled together the various threads of that model under the phrase *Agile law firm*. Author and legal market adviser (and former-colleague) Jordan Furlong describes the model he hopes to see emerge as "a new, adaptive, fit-for-purpose law firm for the 21st century".[29]

In the corporate world the Agile movement has set its sights on replacing the old organisational paradigm – organisations as machines. There is a catch here for the legal world. Most law firm leaders I know would reject an association of their law firm, and law firms in general, with this corporate paradigm. Law firms, according to their view, are

"Agile organisations are designed – and redesigned – for both stability and dynamism."

highly people-centred, culturally rich and emphatically *not* corporate. Following this logic, if law firms were not, in the first place, bureaucratic machine organisations then do they have much need of a new Agile model?

In my experience that view misunderstands the central tenet of the machine organisation which is to prioritise and maintain stability. That is an organisational aim that has been, for decades, absolutely fundamental to how law firms have been run. Law firms, mostly partnerships, can be as rigid a machine as corporates in other sectors – structured in a formalised, top-down way that emphasises the maximisation of shareholder value (in this case, profit per partner).

Agile organisations are designed – and redesigned – for both stability and dynamism. We are not talking here about the ad hoc, constantly shifting and sometimes chaotic way in which some start-ups work; they often lack the stable practices required for a sustainable Agile organisation. The explosion of interest in how to create an Agile model is explained by the fact that in the VUCA world machine organisations that have been built for certainty and stability are at a competitive *disadvantage*. As Eric Ries puts it, "remember, planning is a tool that only works in the presence of a long and stable operating history. And yet, do any of us feel that the world around us is getting more and more stable every day?"[30] That is a statement that should prompt serious reflection in the many law firms who still regard stability, certainty and tradition as among their most valuable assets.

The world of lawyers and law firms is no longer as hermetically sealed and protected as it once was. The bubble in which law firms operated has been burst and is now being impacted by wider trends in real time, rather than very remotely and gradually impacted on a 10-year time lag. The legal market in large jurisdictions, notably England and Wales and Australia, is now fully connected to capital markets – with large law firms bought and sold by private equity and floated on the stock markets. The new war for talent has blown away complacent expectations that a certain cadre of the most intelligent students leaving top universities will inexorably flow into prestige law firms. For many years this top-talent pool has been presented with a whole series of attractive – often better paid – alternatives, especially from an ever-expanding range of technology and financial sub-genres. And the products and outputs of those same crucibles of innovation arrive in our law firms in faster waves of change, disruption and reinvention, creating a continuous digital transformation of legal work that now resembles exactly the revolutionary disruption so many other sectors have experienced before. I call this erosion of legal exceptionalism *the death of difference*.

Two decades ago, some of us in the legal consulting sphere were predicting exactly this digital revolution, but I admit we probably harboured a sense that it was for the profession to come around to and endorse this path. We were a little naïve – lawyers have had very little say in the dramatic digitisation of their profession. The waves of technological – and related economic and societal – change have simply inundated our sandcastle constructs. None of the most powerful people in the law decided this would be a good thing or planned for it. It has happened – is still happening – to the sector regardless of whether we wanted it or not. The shift to Agile is, in large part, about how firms deal with that reality, as some legal pathfinders already are.

Let me just reprise my 10 Agile Attributes from the previous section. Agile law firms, in common with other Agile organisations, are:

- built around highly autonomous teams;
- client-centric;
- constantly innovating and improving;
- insight-driven;
- human;
- fluid and flexible (workplace and workforce);
- organically collaborative;
- restless, radical and challenging;
- digital; and
- united by a common purpose.

Does that sound like your firm? Perhaps it does in parts. Perhaps there is an aspiration to operate that way in some areas, maybe not yet fully realised. If you are starting up your legal services business or have done recently, my hunch is that you might believe that your business is closer to the Agile model than your established law firm competitors. The question you may have to face, however, is whether the Agile characteristics of a small, nimble start-up or scale-up legal firm can be sustained as you grow and maybe bring in more people schooled in traditional law firm systems and behaviours.

In many organisations there is a renewed sense of optimism about their capability for rapid and successful change in the wake of the law's response to the 2020 pandemic. Without a doubt, our industry was able to move mountains in very short timeframes as COVID-19 took hold. We learned a lot about just how far the underlying transformation of the law had already gone, something that many of its citizens had not fully appreciated. Collectively, we got an early peek at a range of very different ways of transacting legal services – an uncanny live trial of what, up until March 2020, had been a speculative future state 'vision'. Not everybody liked what they saw and certainly

"In many organisations there is a renewed sense of optimism about their capability for rapid and successful change in the wake of the law's response to the 2020 pandemic."

not every aspect was positive. Nevertheless, the unique opportunity to experience what the future working in a law firm might look like has stimulated a whole series of debates, decisions and investments around what next. This experience has created more fertile ground for the next phase of Agile transformation.

There are many different paths to agility. Some organisations are born Agile – they use an Agile operating model from the start. Legal start-ups and alternative service providers are taking that approach now. For firms that are already well beyond those early days, becoming Agile is going to involve a *transformation*. Some are already on the journey and I hope this report might help them take the next steps and provide new ideas for acceleration and breaking down residual barriers. Others have barely started and will need to decide whether to tackle the Agile challenge using rapid, powerful waves of change or a steady, systematic emergent route, building from the bottom-up.

Simply rejecting the conventional law firm model does not immediately create an Agile firm. Indeed, many of the examples we could cite from the last decade of alternative departures from the partnership, hourly-billed model have taken a fairly predictable, old-school corporate, machine organisation route. Some of those highly mechanised alternative legal service providers (ALSPs) in high volume, commoditised legal markets, have been successful without really being Agile. Simply being a new entrant or an ALSP does not convey the built-in agility to flex and crest the next wave of change. However, when I look at the full sweep of legal market new entrants, with technology enabled services and products to the fore, there is plenty of evidence of embedded Agile development and project techniques and empowered team structures. While it would be premature to describe any of the Big 4 accounting and consulting firms as Agile organisations today, thanks to their sheer scale, complexity and partnership structure, they are all developing their Agile capabilities at pace. Deloitte, with their huge consulting business, have been particularly adept at strategic pivots and all four firms have demonstrated, in their recent legal practice evolution, the agility with which they are able to scale-up areas of strategic focus.

Leaders who do set out to transform their firm into an Agile model should not expect to achieve this overnight or across the entire firm all at once. Deciding where to start is critical and there is a box at the end of each of the following chapters of the report which suggests the *Agile first steps* firms could take on their journey. An implementation plan is essential, but you should apply Agile principles to how you implement Agile – be prepared to test, iterate and refine as you go.

Addressing the areas where your firm is *least* Agile today is also an important priority. The *Agile first steps* can help you self-assess your current level of organisational agility. If you do not take steps to strengthen the least Agile parts of your firm, your advances in other areas could easily be undermined. I will return to the question of which part(s) of the organisation are right and ripe for piloting the necessary changes and leading the Agile evolution. Those parts could be selected teams or practice groups, or component parts of a business process that operates across all units – or a combination of both.

Agile organisations are flatter, more democractic and more decentralised structures than the command-and-control models that were the default until recently. They are guided by a common purpose to co-create value for all stakeholders. In contrast to an organisation operating like a machine, Agile organisations act like living organisms – a constantly moving, evolving, reacting network of cells. That description prompted me to ask the question: could law firms, in fact, have a head-start and be naturally well-suited to becoming Agile organisations?

Let's take one of Steven Denning's core points about the bureaucratic, machine organisation that Agile is reacting against. He describes its reliance on 'controlism'[31]; highly centralised, top-down management of almost every big decision, investment or product launch. Although law firms have introduced significantly higher levels of business discipline, performance analytics and centralised services over the last two decades, I defy anyone to describe them as bastions of central control. It can be tough for the managing partner, or the executive committee, to make a change really stick around the firm if they don't gain the buy-in and backing of partners. Local offices, different department areas and the teams within them all have a long history of maintaining their own working practices in the face of attempts at firm-wide standardisation. This is by no means always a good thing. But there is a version of the Agile *network of self-managed teams* alive and kicking and, critically, working in the law firm model.

The fact that law firms have some naturally Agile characteristics is hopefully going to prove to be a real asset over the next decade. The restrictive, hallowed and time-honoured fundamentals of the old Boomer generation model – default assumptions like hourly billing, partnership, city office-based workers, service delivery personally by lawyers, with private practice firms not their clients setting the agenda – are being challenged and reimagined.

Basic law firm structures are still built around the fossil outline of their original foundation on partner-led small teams. The small team of the

"Agile organisations are flatter, more democractic and more decentralised structures than the command-and-control models that were the default until recently."

traditional law firm by no means embodies all of the multi-disciplinary characteristics of the Agile team but that shared structural connection can make the transition to an Agile model less difficult for law firms than for many large corporations.

Another natural Agile advantage which law firms possess is that the practice of law is already structured around projects. You may refer to them as engagements or matters, but you are working in an organisation already broken down into defined projects, each with identified stakeholders and some upfront idea of the objective, timescale and key activities and milestones. In that respect a law firm has a lot inherently in common with the world of tech and engineering where the Agile toolkit was born and developed. As I will highlight in the next chapter, the deployment of Agile tools to improve the management and client experience of legal matters, usually referred to as legal project management, is one of the most fundamental tools on your potential journey to agility.

Law firms are always referencing their client focus, client service programmes and client relationships. An Agile consultant hired to introduce the methodology to their first ever law firm might think that this was going to be a pretty easy ride! Unfortunately, the law firm interpretation is not always the same intense, empathetic repositioning of the client at the centre of their organisation that Agile demands. Nevertheless, I believe that most lawyers who engage with the Agile mindset find a natural affiliation with its client-centricity. That makes being client-centred the obvious Agile Attribute to examine first, in the next chapter.

II. Client-centricity

1. Clients at the centre

The impact of globalisation, deregulation and especially the internet have led to a dramatic shift in power in the marketplace from seller to buyer. Steven Denning refers to this switch as the Copernican revolution in management thinking. That is a big statement. He explains that the internet changed everything and: "suddenly the customer was in charge and expected value that was instant, frictionless, intimate, and preferably free".[32]

In his 2017 book, *Law is a Buyer's Market: Building a Client-First Law Firm*, Jordan Furlong identified a problem and one affecting a large proportion of lawyers: "they know that something is happening to their markets and their clients, but they don't have the information or the tools they need to make the necessary adjustments".[33]

Jordan's assessment chimes in with a key plank of my argument in this report. When we worked alongside each other as part of Edge International, we shared a similar take on the future of the profession, albeit one formed from different perspectives – Jordan from Canada and the United States and me from the the United Kingdom and Europe. I want to highlight the very deliberately, perhaps provocatively, chosen title of Jordan's book: *Law is a Buyer's Market*. He explains in detail why he thinks this overdue change in the dynamics of our industry has finally arrived and makes the point that successful law firms of the future will be those able to view absolutely everything through the eyes of, and build their entire business around, their clients.

This client-centred principle is, of course, the founding tenet of Agile organisations. The adoption of Agile thinking and practices across the business is emerging as one of the surest and most comprehensive ways of addressing the need to reorient yourself to the needs of the buyer. As Jordan points out:

> *when we look at the legal market from a seller's perspective, it's almost impossible to imagine why anyone would want to change it. But when we look at it from a buyer's perspective, it's almost impossible to imagine why anyone would want to maintain it.*[34]

Just saying that you are focused on clients or proclaiming that "clients come first" is absolutely not the same as the customer-centric concept at the core of Agile. As Jack Newton, the founder of legal software disrupter Clio and author of *The Client-Centred Law Firm*, points out being client first is not the same as being client-centric.[35]

"*Just saying that you are focused on clients or proclaiming that 'clients come first' is absolutely not the same as the customer-centric concept at the core of Agile.*"

What is the difference? A client-centric firm would answer the following questions positively:

- Does the client's voice and perspective kick-off every important discussion and decision?
- Are your people obsessive about anticipating, meeting and exceeding client expectations?
- Is achieving this the overriding definition of success when performance, reward, promotion or hiring are being considered?

The words that appear in descriptions of client-centred Agile environments are striking and hold significance. These are not just re-treads of generic client service programmes or statements of your ethical-regulatory obligations to clients. Ask yourself if you could describe your people's approach to serving clients using words such as: 'obsessed', 'energised', 'enthusiasm', 'passion', 'delight', 'galvanised'. Don't forget that these words should be applied to your senior leadership and all the organs of firm management as well. The people at the top need to be as client-obsessed as the Agile team members at the front-line.

Agile organisations mobilise *the entire firm* to understand and then meet client needs. The delivery of that service and experience is multi-disciplinary, pulling on every role and function in the firm, very much including the support functions that can still sometimes be disregarded as the 'back-office'. In those areas – IT, finance, HR, risk, document production – law firms can fail to talk about and focus on clients and set client-focused goals. Your support functions should be engaged in client-centred projects and activities and have a clear 'line of sight' from the work they do each day to the value the firm delivers to its clients.

If you are intent upon understanding, engaging with and responding to your clients' needs and objectives, what do you need to do differently? Firms need to ask themselves how they can embed this behaviour at the heart of their organisation and re-engineer the entire organisation around a response to clients' changing needs.

Client intelligence is critical to this process. This goes beyond some stats – fees billed, hours, write-offs, maybe a satisfaction rating – on the latest legal matter you worked on. The intelligence you need to fuel an Agile approach has to tap into the business needs beyond your client's objectives, threats, risks, strategies and people issues. You should gather but also share and regularly update this data. That means providing tools to assist this process and giving lawyers and others permission to invest their time in engaging with clients to gather the intelligence. Once gathered, ensuring that it is used is another challenge. Designing key client dashboards that are available widely across the firm and regularly refreshed and discussed is one way to facilitate this.

The same focus on curiosity needs to be adopted in assessing your firm's performance for the client. Did you deliver, from the client's perspective, what was required? Did you add value? Was your client satisfied? Answering these fundamental questions for any service business, and even more so one setting out to be Agile, is often difficult for law firm leaders to do. The mechanisms which firms use for tracking, reporting and then rewarding performance against the critical metric of meeting client expectations and needs are often too patchy, sometimes non-existent. The fact a client pays your bill, even without grumbles or queries, does not demonstrate that they received the service they wanted. Yet it is, too often, the only indicator a firm can produce to give any sort of answer to the 'did we deliver' question.

Almost certainly, more time is spent on measuring and tracking purely financial by-products from this work and they are much more prominently reported and used in management decision making. This is an early challenge for law firms in setting out on their Agile journey – it is likely that the underpinning structure of goals, values, metrics, principles, processes, systems, reports and incentive needs to be redesigned in order to get the firm to focus on and generate continuous client value.

This is where the make-or-break business case for Agile sits. Continuously delivering more value for your clients. Ideally without having to expend a lot more resource, time and input. This, rather than arbitrary annual fee or profit targets, is the guiding star for the Agile law firm. The financial improvements *flow from* client value improvement, rather than being pursued as a standalone goal that far too often actually conflicts with and undermines efforts to deliver for clients.

I have already used that word 'value' a few times. Client value is the output which justifies all this Agile effort and change. Clients will measure value and prioritise various aspects of it differently, which is the reason for so much emphasis on getting a much deeper insight into your clients. Financial outcomes, including value for money, are likely to be a component part. But business outcomes, risk mitigation, wise counsel, emotional support, simple responsiveness to queries and 'making me look good' (a phrase often used in relation to general counsel as clients – what will make the GC look good?) will often be part of the answer too. In many areas of law, winning the case will of course be important. Value will typically be some mix of outcome and experience. Until you engage more deeply with clients you won't be able to say for sure what that mix is.

"The fact a client pays your bill, even without grumbles or queries, does not demonstrate that they received the service they wanted. Yet it is, too often, the only indicator a firm can produce to give any sort of answer to the 'did we deliver' question."

There is a permanent 'win/win' which underpins the success of Agile organisations giving both value for the client and value (ultimately monetisable) for your firm. These two outcomes are umbilically linked. Clients and customers are willing to pay more for the products and services they really love. They will return to and be willing to spend more with firms that deliver exactly what they are looking for.

You are going to have to establish early on in your Agile journey which clients you are focusing on. Few law firms serve a single, homogenous client group. Most firms have multiple practice areas, often serving both companies and individuals. As firms grow the range of clients they serve extends, spreading across regions, then borders, and embracing multiple industry sectors and segments. Trying to 'focus' on this spectrum all at once will result in frustration.

Start with your primary client market and identify their common characteristics. You can move onto addressing other client groups by bringing other teams who serve these clients into the process and by extending the lessons and successes you have with the first group. I am definitely not suggesting you pick off one part of your client base and only ever focus on them. But do start *somewhere* rather than *everywhere*. Or *nowhere!*

Getting started on that deeper understanding of your clients is critical to advancing your organisational agility. Throughout this report I will feature a series of tools, some briefly and some in more depth, that will support the Agile transition. Over the following pages I will begin with some valuable tools for client understanding and engagement.

> **Agile toolkit – client journey mapping**
>
> Understanding the client journey is a good starting point for any Agile initiative. Never lose sight of the central principle here – you are following the client's journey, through their eyes and using their language, and not the journey of an instruction or a document through your firm. The two intersect but they are not the same. The client begins their journey needing some legal advice before your firm knows about it or begins working with them. And they will end that journey, most likely, sometime after you have completed your work and sent them a bill.
>
> The most important ingredient to bring to any analysis of the client journey is empathy. It is a much-used word. Its meaning today is captured well by the old saw that to really understand another person you should 'walk a mile in their shoes'. This can be tough for any busy professional to do, especially after years of doing similar work for apparently similar clients. Professionals are steeped in the perspectives, structured education, culture and intense workload of their chosen career. As law firms get larger, they also build routines, processes, language and metrics that tend to focus the attention internally. There is often little institutional interest displayed in the motivation or specific situation of individual clients. It is very easy to lose sight of the fact that the task your team is carrying out may be something they have done 30 times this week already, but the client has possibly never experienced before. Bringing empathy across your entire firm is perhaps one of the biggest changes you will face in taking this route.
>
> If your firm can bring together empathy, a curious, open attitude and smart analysis and focus them on the client journey you will discover a huge amount more about your clients' actual experience of working with you. This exercise is client journey mapping. Creating these maps is akin to the work you would undertake to create a process map. The key difference is two-fold. First, you will engage far more directly with clients (and former clients) to populate the client journey map; you should avoid guessing or inputting their perspective by proxy. Secondly, you will focus more attention on clients' emotional and personal responses to each step on the journey.
>
> Client journey maps are built up from each touchpoint or interaction you have with them, with additional detail drawn from the client's

II. Client-centricity

"Getting started on that deeper understanding of your clients is critical to advancing your organisational agility."

other experiences throughout the conduct of their particular transaction. For example, in a typical house purchase the purchaser will also engage with real estate agents, mortgage brokers, banks, removal firms and others, and in actions that do not involve you as their lawyer. You should add these activities into the client journey map, to build as complete and accurate a picture of the overall journey as possible.

The first touchpoint a prospective client has with your firm is unlikely to be reading and signing an engagement letter. You need to begin much earlier and not fall into the obvious trap of assuming the journey begins when the matter is opened. Indeed, the ideal journey start-point is as the client first recognises that they have an issue which might require legal advice. Their first interaction with your firm is possibly going to be through seeing advertising, a webpage, a directory entry and then through your switchboard. A good client journey map will have a number of stages even before a proposal or quote is issued.

It is hard to build maps at the right level of detail if you are trying to cover too large a piece of the firm in one exercise. Focusing on a specific type of work and client group will yield more value and insight.

As noted, this is a great place to start in trying to expose your clients' experience and begin to apply Agile principles to your firm. There are some very good resources available that will help you dig deeper into how to undertake this work. Do not assume that the mapping process requires a huge amount of time and effort or specialist resources. You will need to lean on the team members who work in that practice area and engage those clients for their unique knowledge of how things work but you can build the map organically as you collect their input. There are plenty of materials available on customer or client journey mapping but I would recommend law firms take a closer look at Part 2 of Jack Newton's *The Client Centered Law Firm*.[36]

Agile toolkit – jobs to be done theory

One technique that is widely used in product-centred industries is known as 'jobs to be done' (JTBD). Simply put, JTBD is based on the idea that your clients are not buying a product or service from you, they are hiring you to get a job done. The question is whether you really understand what that job is. Once again, this tool puts the emphasis on empathy. Only by looking beyond what it is you think they are buying – ie looking down the supplier lens – and tapping into the underlying result your client is looking to achieve, can you ensure that you deliver the right product or service. Most Agile tools that I explore in this report help with how to design and deliver the best product or service. JTBD focuses more on what product or service to deliver.

I think the most viewed and best recognised PowerPoint slide in legal management history might be the slide used for many years by Professor Richard Susskind to illustrate the point behind JTBD. It simply shows a hole in a wall. Susskind explains that one of the world's largest power tool manufacturers uses this slide with its people: "this", they tell their audience, "is what we sell". The hole is the job that the customer needs doing. The drill is just the means to that end. The same principle applied to legal services can often open up a universe of client experiences and priorities that it is otherwise hard for lawyers to know about. Busy lawyers do not habitually ask the right questions that will reveal what the client's JTBD really is.

JTBD is applied to enhance the depth and accuracy of your definition of what the client needs and wants, in the initial phases of most of the other Agile models featured in the report (eg, empathise and define phases of design thinking or define stages in Lean Sigma, Legal Project Management etc). These are often called *user stories* in Agile language (you will read more about these later in this report). A simple three-part structure is used to describe the client's triggering event or situation, their motivation and goal, and their desired outcome:

When _____ , I want to _____ , so I can _____ .

An example would be:

> When I need to sign a legal document in relation to my case, I want to be able to do that very quickly without hassle or confusion, so I can get on with my life confident it has been dealt with correctly.

The job story should not suggest fixed solutions, specific products or technologies. In the example above, e-signature software looks like a potentially great solution, but it may not work for everybody or for this type of legal work; so we have not jumped to the conclusion that "to do that very quickly without hassle or confusion" should read "to use e-signing technology". The subject of your job story is always the client – or end user if this is an internal job – and *not* the people delivering or developing the service. Keep them out of your job definition. As will become clear by the end of this report, these tools can provide guide rails to force your people to think from the client's perspective, truly empathising, rather than slipping back into their own service provider viewpoint.

This is a very quick dip into JTBD theory intended to get you thinking about how important it is to think beyond your immediate focus on the service or product you are delivering and truly empathise with and understand the client's motivation and desired outcome.

2. Legal project management

I am devoting a sizeable chunk of this chapter to explaining and examining how the ideas and tools that are usually tagged as legal project management (LPM) can help law firms advance their Agile programme. There are four good reasons for this focus on methodologies that I acknowledge are not new and which some law firms may have tried and found hard to implement or extract significant value from. First, the fact that LPM has established itself and has been tried and tested in multiple law firms around the world is a big plus – this is a practical tool for your Agile journey that we already *know* can be adopted to legal work. As Steven ter Horst, Head of Innovation and Knowledge at leading Dutch firm Houthoff put it responding to my request for comments on the use of LPM, "you could argue that law firms have worked in an 'Agile' fashion before it was even called Agile".

"LPM is the application of best practices in project management to the delivery of legal services. In the classic business definition, a project is a 'temporary endeavour undertaken to accomplish a unique purpose'."

Second, LPM is inherently client-centred. The project best practices incorporated into LPM begin with the project (or matter) goals and outcomes for the client. Third, successful LPM initiatives lead to dramatically improved levels of transparency in the working relationship between firm and client (and, often, between different lawyers working inside your firm) – something that is fundamental to the Agile way of working. Finally, LPM uses post-matter debriefs to systemise a cycle of rapid and continuous reflection, improvement and learning. In doing so it takes aim directly at a common failing in over-busy law firm environments.

Those four factors make LPM a skeleton around which the Agile law firm can be built. The LPM methodology has absorbed many ideas that emerged from the Agile development movement and many key features are shared with other specific tools including Scrum and Lean.

The early 2020s seems likely to be the 'tipping point' moment when LPM becomes commonplace and when partners, lawyers and clients start to actively seek out – even compete for – legal project managers to coordinate their matters, rather than the LPM team chasing down work. But there is still a way to go, with many firms at the start of their journey.

I recommend every firm explores the benefits of LPM. It is hard to identify a credible reason not to invest some of the firm's time and energy into developing a standard, agile, client-centric model for managing all matters. A fully integrated LPM approach increases the chances of success, where LPM is fully aligned with, connected to and supported by every part of the firm. That includes not just legal teams but also finance, HR/people, knowledge management, marketing and IT.

LPM established itself as an important lawyer tool over the last decade. In the first years of the 2010s, only the largest firms, mostly in North America, had begun to adopt LPM standards and employ the initial crop of project managers, in response to growing corporate client pressure. Most firms across the globe did not know what the LPM acronym stood for and their clients were not exhibiting interest, let alone applying pressure. The global spread of LPM and its dissemination down through the tiers of the legal market are still relatively recent phenomena.

LPM is the application of best practices in project management to the delivery of legal services. In the classic business definition, a project is a "temporary endeavour undertaken to accomplish a unique purpose". All projects have a beginning, a middle and an end. A legal case, matter or transaction fits the definition of a project and should be well suited to the application of project management best practice. In reality, lawyers have been suspicious of techniques that were originally developed to ensure the smooth running of construction, technology or large government projects and had traditionally tended to prefer much softer, less defined and precise 'matter management' guidelines.

Before the wider adoption of LPM, firms were accustomed to managing even their largest client engagements and transactions without explicitly recognising that these were projects where enterprise grade project management skills and standards, adopted from sectors well beyond the boundaries of legal work, can be applied to great effect. Although experienced lawyers managed matters and often did so well, this was *accidental* project management. As legal projects became larger, more complex and often more international, law firms and their clients saw more need to bring greater coordination, communication, planning and monitoring to bear on legal projects.

A combination of that increasing complexity, commoditisation and fee pressure led larger corporate clients, initially in the United States, to question whether this well-meaning amateur approach to bet-the-company legal projects was truly effective. Clients began to challenge their external counsel on this and have continued to do so through most of the last decade. More clients have joined the movement to see effective project management introduced into the legal sector and found themselves allied to the first wave of dedicated legal project managers hired into law firms and to the increasingly aligned aspirations of some progressive firm management teams.

LPM was initially a principally manual activity, aided where possible by home-made adaptation of basic tech tools such as Excel and MS Project. More recently, a mini-industry of matter management, scoping, pricing and legal project applications has been spawned. More large firms are now using these systems to support their LPM. Project applications do deliver new levels of accuracy, transparency and granularity into the interface between law firm and client on the scoping, resourcing and pricing of matters, whether that technology is applied at the procurement and pricing stage, constantly throughout the course of the engagement or when billing (particularly through the now widespread use of eBilling and legal spend management applications).

LPM is routinely applied to manage fixed fee and alternative fee arrangement (AFA) matters, where the firm has a fee budget or cap and can boost profitability through improved management of matters. But LPM also has an important role to play in hourly priced matters where clients are increasingly wary and unsure whether firms are genuinely prioritising efficiency and delivering value. In some cases, clients will be using eBilling or legal spend analytics tools to scrutinise the firm's performance on a time basis. LPM can help firms to gain and retain the trust of their clients, as well as to minimise invoice rejections, complaints and fee write-offs.

Just as importantly, a wide LPM programme can contribute to improving lawyer utilisation, ensuring that scarce and expensive lawyer resources are properly planned, managed, monitored and allocated.

3. Legal project management today

LPM is by no means universally accepted or adopted in law firms today. A common response of lawyers to the introduction of project management ideas has often been to protest that legal matters require very different, more nuanced skills and approaches to project management in other industries. This line of argument has not died out entirely, but most firms that have seriously introduced LPM, and certainly most corporate clients, would disagree.

Nevertheless, many readers may recognise an attitude that still survives in parts of their own firm. One aim of this report is to spread greater understanding of Agile tools and techniques that are already in use in the legal profession and help law firms overcome the residual resistance to using them as a core component of client service and delivery. I believe that no client-centred law firm can afford to move forward without a carefully developed and then rapidly deployed plan for achieving a great standard of LPM right across their firm.

A high percentage of corporate and government clients now demand to know exactly how their law firms are going to scope, plan and manage their legal projects, often upfront at pitch or panel review stage. The ubiquity of LPM as a commercial client expectation has been accelerated by the rise of in-house networks and collaboration vehicles such as the Corporate Legal Operations Consortium (CLOC)[37] and the Association of Corporate Counsel (ACC).[38]

A survey of legal project managers conducted in the first half of 2019, by the International Institute of Legal Project Management (IILPM) highlighted the growth of both legal project manager roles and LPM usage. It also picked up on continued concerns that engaging the wider lawyer population with LPM was still lagging behind the potential. IILPM Member Antony Smith summarised the findings in an article[39]:

- 72% of legal project managers responding worked in law firms specialising in commercial and business law – an unsurprising

"LPM is routinely applied to manage fixed fee and alternative fee arrangement (AFA) matters, where the firm has a fee budget or cap and can boost profitability through improved management of matters."

figure perhaps, but note the substantial minority that don't work in those typically 'Big Law' firms;
- there is a common perception that many of the practising lawyers in responding firms still do not understand or appreciate the role that legal project managers can play;
- only 28% of legal project managers felt they were involved early enough in matters to help define scope and only 33% were confident they were regarded as the primary point of contact for all operational issues they work on;
- further education of practising lawyers is needed about what legal project management is, the role of legal project managers and how to get the best out of them;
- 50% of respondents who class themselves as practising lawyers felt they have sufficient control over resources during matters. This drops to just 25% of legal project managers;
- a majority of respondents reported that project kick-off meetings (68% overall) and post-project reviews (62% of legal project managers) regularly take place;
- 28% of legal project manager respondents have been in their role for five years or more, underlining the emergence of an LPM career route.

Agile toolkit – an Agile LPM framework
Project management teaches us that as soon as an engagement exists with a specific required outcome, a start and end date, and a budget, it constitutes a project that needs to be planned, organised and controlled. This is the case whether the piece of client work is simple or complicated, short term or long term, single-handed or multi-lawyered. In the context of legal work, the simple model for project management divides projects into four or five distinct but overlapping phases of operation.

A good example of a four-phase model is the LPM framework developed by a group of specialists who together formed the International Institute of Legal Project Management (IILPM).[40] Another has been published by the hugely influential Corporate Legal Operations Consortium (CLOC),[41] which has synthesised a lot of LPM thinking to develop its own guide for in-house legal teams. This assists the management of internal business client expectations and requirements, while also managing the law firms and other external vendors who might be brought into these engagements. These four-phase models break down into the following phases:

- define/intake
- plan/planning
- deliver/execution
- close/review

Some LPM models have evolved to five phases, including an extra phase before the final closure and evaluation phase. This 'monitor' phase covers monitoring and measuring. In this phase, progress of the project is monitored and scope creep, bottlenecks and other inefficiencies are eradicated. The matter budget is tracked and any necessary adjustments – communicated to and agreed with the client – are made. Adding in this phase brings this essential ongoing activity to the fore, helping highlight a critical component of good project management that can often be ignored or skimmed through in legal work. But it is not strictly a sequential phase; there is not a period of time toward the end of a project when all the monitoring gets done.

I use my own variation on the five-phase Agile LPM model in my work with law firms which does pull out monitoring and reporting in order to give it greater focus and attention. This model has the following phases and is illustrated below:

- scope
- plan
- execute
- monitor
- evaluate

Figure 1. Five-phase Agile LPM model

Phase	Scope	Plan	Execute	Monitor	Evaluate
Stage	Definition	Planning	Execution	Monitoring	Review and close
Deliverables	Understand client needs; Scoping; Outline pricing; SLAs/terms	Resourcing; Timetabling; Budgeting; Comms; Contingency planning	Internal/externals comms; Resource decisions; Collaborative working	Measuring and reporting against time, scope, cost and handling variations and changes	Post-matter review, what went well and lessons learned

Taking a slightly closer look at each of the phases will help you connect the LPM methodology with the way your firm is working with clients and with the wider Agile management model.

Project Phase One – scope (initiation and scoping)

While projects can go wrong at every phase, the first phase is critical for setting the expectations of all the stakeholders and the client, defining the client's problem and needs, and clarifying agreed-upon objectives, expected outcomes and benefits to the client. The initial set of meetings with both the client and other internal teams and resources and the development of a scope of works are of critical importance in order to ensure that everybody is on the same page.

Best practice, therefore, requires the entire scope of the engagement to be agreed upon and recorded in writing from the very start. With input from the client and other interested parties, there should be a summary of the purpose of the engagement and expected outputs.

Law firms must take great care at the initiation phase to match the client's needs with a realistic and agreed-upon fees budget. Jobs to be done theory, which was discussed above, comes into play here. This can be tricky, especially where the client team includes representatives with differing needs. As Woldow and Richardson put it: "the general counsel's highest priority, for example, might be exhausting all possible legal avenues and risks. Meanwhile, the CFO is fixated on minimizing legal costs and outside legal spend, the chief compliance officer thinks impeccable compliance is more important than taking entrepreneurial risk, the chief procurement officer wants to select the lowest bidder, and the business head protests any activity not keyed to furthering business objectives".[42]

Clients want a number of Agile outcomes from their lawyers that successful LPM projects should deliver on:

- value as defined by the clients, rather than the firm;
- efficient management of their matter;
- legal spending within budget and, ideally, reducing year-on-year;
- spend and outcome predictability and no surprises;
- timely and responsive communication;
- a deep understanding of the client, their needs and their businesses; and
- alignment of the client and the firm's interests.

It is vital to agree with the client at this stage not only the work to be included in the scope but also work that will fall outside the scope and will be dealt with by a separate fee agreement. One of the keys to successful fixed-fee quotes is the ability of the law firm to define caveats and exclusions clearly and then proactively deal with *change orders* as unforeseen events occur. It is good practice to agree with the client that out-of-scope work will not be commenced until and unless the client agrees.

The initiation and scoping phase is also the point to identify possible risks that need to be controlled, monitored, mitigated or eradicated. For example, the risk to the client of fighting a dispute or of pursuing a risky tax strategy needs to be evaluated, taking into consideration the client's risk appetite and the probability and potential impact of that risk factor arising.

Project Phase Two – plan
The scope phase ought to have produced initial outlines for staffing, tasks, timelines, budgets and deliverables. The plan phase turns those outlines into a working plan that is firmly centred on the agreed-upon outcome and delivering client value and sets out the matter strategy and action plan in some detail. All project plans have both external components that track key client activities and internal components that relate primarily to how the firm does the work.

In substantial engagements, this plan phase can be extensive and time-consuming, but in smaller or routine matters it can be completed in a very short time. In larger matters, much can be accomplished by brainstorming the planning at an early project team meeting, which can also help to identify unrealistic or missing assumptions. Later, I will take a closer look at the value of using Kanban methods as a basis for this planning work, for both simple and complex matters.

It can be helpful to include the client directly in the plan phase, as early dialogue helps with testing and refining the overall plan. Some clients now require their engagements or projects to be broken down into designated component parts. Getting the plan right will help ensure the execution of the project on time, on budget and at the expected level of quality. The plan is also the most effective vehicle for communicating the dimensions of the project to all team members and keeping everyone aligned.

Law firms do get criticised for failure to plan appropriately, but there is a danger of overplanning. As LPM guru Steven Levy states: "Extending planning beyond a reasonable point is not an efficient use of time or budget; the value such additional planning adds is less than the cost to do the additional work ... it's the project team that will pay for analysis paralysis. Work gets pushed up against deadlines because the team is waiting on the project manager for decisions."[43]

The project plan should be documented and then updated regularly. Major parts of it should be accessible to the client. A member of the project team should be tasked with responsibility of maintaining and updating the plan. Technology can also play a role – many firms have developed custom proprietary software, while others use popular project management packages such as Basecamp. These applications help you organise team collaboration, create calendars and Gantt charts, sequentially assign tasks, map dependencies and collect documents.

A fee quote or estimate will have been agreed during the scope phase, but in the plan phase it is important that the fees budget is broken down into projections and milestones for the various phases and tasks. These can be converted into key performance indicators and targets. Whether the firm is working to a fixed quotation or an estimated guideline, it is vital that the project manager keeps a close eye on all billable time recorded against the project and individual phases.

At this point, as the overall project timeline and plan is broken down into phases and tasks, the team can also utilise Agile concepts and identify how the project can be deconstructed into user stories, each with defined client outcomes, and sprints, which I examine in more detail in the next section. A contract project breakdown could, for example, include sprints for draft, negotiate, approve, execute.

Project Phase Three – execute
Many clients will be as focused on how their projects are managed, controlled and coordinated as on the technical legal work itself, which they often take for granted will be performed to a high-quality standard. In the context of LPM, the execute phase calls for the project manager to be more the conductor of the orchestra than one of the instrumentalists, though many legal project managers will simultaneously be doing legal work on the project.

Legal work often starts before the plan phase has been fully concluded. Therefore, the execute phase will almost always overlap with the plan phase. The critical thing you need to ensure is that someone remains in clear overall control. Clients often cite poor delegation as a common complaint about law firms. They do not expect (and do not want to pay for) partners being involved all the time, but they do want partners to step in when needed, to be accessible and to have a good grip on the engagement generally.

Overall project control requires strong leadership. The legal project manager will often be a lawyer. After all, LPM is all about delivering excellent legal services and that will encompass your engagement strategy, supervision and quality control. However, the project management skills, as opposed to legal technical skills, that are required in order to lead a complex legal project should not be underestimated and legal project managers increasingly have advanced project qualifications.

Project managers use Agile staples such as daily stand-ups to provide very focused, disciplined and efficient routines for the team to combat blockages and ensure the smooth and seamless execution of their work.

Project Phase Four – monitor
Proper monitoring and rapid remediation of the project is critical. The project manager needs to monitor consistently to know if project tasks and targets are running to plan. Agile project management techniques like sprints and daily stand-ups can provide rigour to monitoring and management. Any adjustments need to be made quickly and in good time with the client's involvement where necessary. Many firms now use sophisticated dashboards that clearly illustrate the state of play in terms of completed tasks and activities, billings to date by phase, work in progress and time spent by team members. Tracking all these metrics is vital not just to control the fees budget but to ensure that deadlines and milestones promised to clients are met. Where the firm has no sophisticated system to track progress, the project leader must rely on a more manual process, maybe including Kanban boards.

"Many firms now use sophisticated dashboards that clearly illustrate the state of play in terms of completed tasks and activities, billings to date by phase, work in progress and time spent by team members."

Project Phase Five – evaluate

No project can properly end unless there is a sign-off – the moment when the client makes an explicit or implicit declaration that the engagement has been properly concluded and that project outcomes have been achieved to the client's satisfaction. This is clearly also the phase when final invoices are prepared, submitted and paid.

An in-depth debrief with the client is not just nice to have – it plays an important part in the firm's future relationships with them. An internal debrief is also an essential element of legal projects, but is too often ignored. A simple but highly effective internal debrief agenda has just three items on it – what went well; what did not go so well; what we learned from the project.

This is a chance to review, preserve and capitalise on documentation drawn up in the course of the project. If the firm is to resist reinventing the wheel on every project, then any useful precedents, checklists and documents need to be captured in the firm's know-how systems. The insight gained through doing this final phase of LPM right can be utilised to create significant, permanent improvement in the way the firm works. That cycle of continuous improvement is pure Agile, running detailed retrospectives after each sprint and project. The Agile commitment to continuous learning and to acting on problems identified in retrospectives is an important behaviour for firms to adopt.

Finally, the conclusion of the engagement gives an opportunity both to celebrate success, perhaps with a team celebration, and for the project manager and lawyers involved in the project to give constructive positive feedback to team members.

Agile toolkit – Kanban and LPM tools

A wide range of different variations on LPM are in use across the legal world. I have come across plenty of home-grown and bought-in protocols, models, systems and tools being used with success. Some are simple and local – for example, the use of software basics such as Excel and MS Office Tasks to manage projects in particular teams. Others are more sophisticated and coordinated firmwide programmes. Neither route is right or wrong, though it is seldom a good idea to try a big bang firmwide roll-out before first piloting, testing and refining the use of LPM on a smaller scale.

Many firms still have undeveloped infrastructure and technology in this area, as it has not been a major priority. There are significant opportunities for legal software developers, including but not restricted to the big practice management system providers, to come up with seamless, easy to learn and use products which allow legal project managers to perform their key tasks, especially those of cost tracking and reporting. Where tools do exist, there is some evidence that firms are wary and not convinced by their capabilities, with take-up running quite slowly up to 2020.

LPM tools and functions work best if integrated into underlying practice management, time recording and business intelligence tools, creating fully integrated platforms. Tasks and activities identified in the LPM plan will cascade into pre-populated time sheets and dashboards for the firm and its clients. I am now beginning to see this extend to task assignments, aided by availability and experience data points easily visible within the platform, something being introduced into large law firms using products such as Mason & Cook's Vantage application (now part of the BigHand legal software stable).

Examples of LPM tools in use
Kanban/Lean: most consultants working in this area would agree that the 'full-fat' version of Lean, popularised and widely used in manufacturing environments, is difficult to translate successfully to legal and professional work. However, various approaches derived from Lean principles have been used with some success in law firms. I will take a look at some of these other adaptations in the following chapter on continuously innovating and improving.

In particular, the use of Kanban boards, a tool used in Lean, has struck a chord with lawyers and this comparatively 'light Agile' methodology is being successfully used in a range of firms around the globe (and not just in North America – other examples include leading firms Tilleke & Gibbins, in Thailand, and Clayton Utz, in Australia). Many lawyers have a visual preferred learning style and that goes some way to explaining the relative popularity of Kanban as a tool.

Kanban can be summed up into five principles or goals:

- visualise workflow;
- limit work in progress;
- measure and manage flow;
- make process policies explicit; and
- use models to recognise process improvement opportunities.

If you are not following all of these principles, then you might have a Kanban board but you will not have a Kanban system.

As outlined at the start of this report, the Kanban 'just in time' methodology was developed at Toyota and initially applied to manufacturing production management. However, over the last few decades, these techniques have been deployed again and again in business sectors a long way from the original factory floor.

In the legal and professional world, the basic building blocks of Kanban boards have been adopted by many organisations and are sometimes rebadged matter-management boards. The principal features of the use of Kanban boards in a law firm setting are:

- Kanban boards can be used to manage and collaborate on your legal projects. These boards are typically split into three simple columns (*To Do, Doing* and *Done*) and provide a quick visual status update with the use of physical or digital task cards to track your progress.
- Complex technology isn't required to operate a matter management board, especially where the project team are all co-located. A wall, roll of paper or whiteboard, sticky notes and marker pens are all you need, which makes these boards a good, easy way of getting started on LPM.
- However, as you move on to tackle projects that extend across locations and teams or visualise multiple projects being run within the team (or just run out of wall-space), firms can use one of the software systems designed to maintain and share digital matter management boards. Needless to say, these digital applications have come into their own in the remote working world that dawned in spring 2020, although many Kanban users believe that the compelling visual impact of the physical Kanban board has been sorely missed. Firms have deployed various tools to visualise and plan complex matters. I have seen law firms using popular cross-industry tools including Microsoft Planner (often connected into Teams channels), Trello, Asana and Smartsheet. You can add, allocate and reschedule tasks easily and team members are notified when a task is assigned to them. Everyone can see the current status of the matter in real-time.
- Tasks are represented as cards which are physically moved left to right through columns representing the different phases of a process. This simple tool can provide an immediate, up-to-date view of the status and progress of a matter.
- Drilling deeper into matters is also straightforward – the single column headed-up 'Doing' is extended out into multiple columns representing sequential phases, creating a more detailed and informative breakdown of the actual delivery phase of the matter. For litigation matters, for example, these additional columns would follow the main phases prescribed by local procedure rules, around which your firm's contentious cases are structured.

"It makes sense that Kanban is often regarded as an essential component of any legal Agile or LPM roll-out – it provides a highly visual, collaborative and engaging focal point for the new way of working."

- The Kanban board technique is inherently action-orientated, with team meetings often held around the board and focused on the clearly displayed activity information. Problems and backlogs can be tackled immediately around the board.
- Team-working is also deepened by use of the Kanban boards and cards; with the whole team workload suddenly visible to all and capable of being reviewed, discussed and addressed *in situ*. To an extent, the same applies to electronic Kanban/Agile project tools, which allow the whole team to see the current status of tasks and matters. It makes sense that Kanban is often regarded as an essential component of any legal Agile or LPM roll-out – it provides a highly visual, collaborative and engaging focal point for the new way of working.

Project collaboration platforms: A large team of lawyers communicating with clients and among themselves through email is inefficient and potentially insecure. Long email discussions, randomly forwarded and copied to other people, often contain important data and attachments and they result in team members wondering if they have the latest version/data and searching through their inboxes. A well-structured and well-used project collaboration site, where documents and other content can be uploaded, shared, drafted and commented on, is more efficient and delivers a single source of truth 24/7. There has been a proliferation of these tools in recent years, led by Thomson Reuters' HighQ product. Many firms are now developing the inherent features of Microsoft Teams to support collaboration.

Case management office (CMO): one way to enable, deliver and drive value through a more widespread use of LPM in law firms is to create a CMO, based on a central programme management office (PMO) in the corporate world. The debate about departmental or central LPM is still ongoing and both can work well, depending on your firm's need, environment, size and maturity. A CMO can provide governance, control, efficiently allocated project management resources and standard methodology. That methodology can include templates, tools, techniques, resourcing, education, knowledge management, quality assurance and project oversight metrics. Some larger firms have functions responsible for overseeing the application of LPM in their firm, often alongside pricing or a broader 'legal operations' remit. They can support the initial scoping and pricing stages but also utilise actual matter performance data to analyse how teams are performing against those initial plans and quotes as part of the monitor activity.

Deal and litigation checklists: a tool to get started with LPM quickly and cheaply is by building a checklist, along Kanban lines. These can be fairly simple Excel or even Word checklist templates. Microsoft Outlook Tasks are used by some lawyers, although this has limitations as more team members are added and collaboration is at a premium.

After-action reviews (retrospectives): a large number of law firms already stipulate, at least in principle, mandatory after-action reviews or debriefs, particularly for larger matters. Some of the frameworks in place in firms are excellent and lawyers across the firm are shepherded, supported and chased-up by passionate and persuasive knowledge or compliance professionals. In my experience, unfortunately, the percentage of after-action reviews that are completed and then followed up and converted into improvement action is small. An LPM programme puts greater emphasis on this valuable activity as an embedded element of how legal teams work. As with any change to working practices that involves effort and thought, you will need to sell the 'what's in it for me' benefits hard. That is another reason why I always advocate a proof of concept trial in specific areas of the firm first.

Project initiation (or scoping) documents (PID): formally define the matter by describing the goal, strategy, working methods, organisation and interfaces with other parties and documenting this in a standard-form PID. Using smart document automation tools to create PIDs quickly and easily from onboarding data and a small amount of other data input is now feasible and could transform the clear communication of project scope and plans around extended, virtual teams.

Matter planning and budgeting software: a range of matter management applications are available to law firms. These provide tools that lawyers can use for setting and then tracking performance against milestones, activities and responsible parties/resources. Ideally, they will integrate cost and time reporting to track and monitor performance against plan.

Project/matter management training: many firms kick-off LPM roll-outs with a training programme. I have already advised that it is best to pilot LPM first, but when you feel ready to tackle a wider programme starting with education is a sensible option. Firms have typically begun by offering all partners or all lawyers professional project management training. In some cases, this is more selective and sometimes backed up by formal project management accreditation for identified 'legal project managers'. I would caution firms not to exclude secretarial and support staff from this training and to also ensure that those working in related business functions such as finance, risk and knowledge are also trained – implemented successfully LPM, and Agile more broadly, will have a significant impact on their roles too.

"The debate about departmental or central LPM is still ongoing and both can work well, depending on your firm's need, environment, size and maturity."

4. The role of the legal project manager

The organic development of LPM as outlined above is now set to combine with big legal technology trends and the dramatic digital acceleration we saw in the wake of the pandemic to produce a new, much more universal strain of LPM for the 2020s. What is beginning to happen is the leveraging of machine learning, intuitive and very flexible user apps and the disciplines and tools of knowledge management to transform LPM into a highly tech-enabled tool for streamlining legal workflows, utilising the latest technology innovation and enabling transparent, real-time and collaborative communication between client and law firm. In the spirit of Agile this tool will adapt and develop constantly.

I have interviewed a number of highly experienced LPM practitioners about the current state and future development of LPM. Sarah Barrett-Vane has held senior legal operations roles and is now a consultant with in-house teams and law firms. She believes that "the very fact that most people in the legal sector (both private practice and in-house teams) now know what LPM is and the benefits it brings – to both sides – is the biggest trend". The rise in job advertisements and professional networks tells her that LPM is "an actual career path now, as is legal operations". Antony Smith, founder of Legal Project Management Limited, agrees:

> *the number of legal project manager roles advertised continues to grow, and legal project management is now very well established in the larger private practice law firms and in-house legal departments ... becoming a legal project manager is a viable long-term career option.*

You don't have to be a lawyer to be a legal project manager. Law firms are filled with legal subject matter experts, but they do need solid project management added to their legal teams to deliver exceptional service and this has started happening. Adding in this diversity of thought is valuable when solving complex client problems and an obvious application of Agile multi-disciplinary team principles. The addition of exceptional project professionals, who are not lawyers but are gifted and proven problem solvers, adds to the mix of skills law firms have on their team.

In larger firms and on large matters, this multi-skilled approach, under the direction of legal project managers, is going further, with client teams comprising lawyers, project managers, data scientists, process redesign professionals, finance and technology specialists all working together. Your firm may not have people with these skills on your payroll, but you might still be able to find new ways of accessing and collaborating with these specialists and deploying genuinely diverse, multi-disciplinary teams on major client engagements.

Antony Smith delivers the UK training and certification provided by the International Institute of Legal Project Management (IILPM) and also believes we are about to see a switch to a position where demand for LPM support and resources starts to outstrip supply:

> *alumni from large law firms who re-visit my course to explain their day-to-day LPM work report that increasingly they are being approached by lawyers asking for help and that they do not have to chase work. This is not evenly distributed and experienced yet though.*[44]

The single biggest takeaway from the IILPM survey was that further education of practising lawyers is still required so that they understand more clearly what legal project management is and how to work best with legal project managers.[45]

In the next few years, the most sophisticated firms look likely to establish more formal strategic account management (SAM) teams as a further evolution of LPM for their key clients. These SAM teams will be focused intently on constantly communicating and working with those key clients and will be able to identify expectations, preferences and factors that will influence scope, time and cost prior to matters even beginning.

The next phase for LPM in law firms may also see the location of the LPM resource centralised and moved away from physical co-location in large city offices. With many US and UK headquartered firms already running a nearshore, low-cost centre, project management is one of a number of components of legal work that could switch to these locations or, especially post-COVID, be operated from just about anywhere as it becomes prohibitively expensive to run ever bigger LPM teams out of those big city offices. Firms with growing teams of legal project managers are already engaged in the task of re-engineering their work so that it can be delivered competitively by paralegals/specialists at lower regional rates and performed remotely and digitally. The trade-off for lawyers and their clients is that they get more attention and intensive management of the matter for no increase in project management cost. Firms that already do this have an immediate competitive advantage – others will simply have to follow.

5. Implementing LPM – should we apply LPM essentials to every client matter?

In the first wave of the LPM programme roll-out most people assumed LPM should be reserved for large, complex, often multi-lawyer and sometimes multi-jurisdiction matters. But most matters do not look like this. Many lawyers and firms don't generally work on such large engagements and, based on that assumption, won't engage with or reap the benefits of using LPM techniques. Surely, applying LPM to smaller matters and a wider range of clients has real value, even in areas where clients have not to-date been demanding it?

I think the answer to that question is a resounding 'yes', though I acknowledge that full-scale LPM programmes and standing LPM teams are not easy to cost-justify where lower value and margin work predominates. Also, clients, as well as the internal lawyer team, will become quickly frustrated if additional layers of administration and time/cost are introduced. However, applying project best practice and Agile principles to every service you provide to clients is a competitive battleground for the modern law firm. I believe that rolling out LPM is your most effective route to creating the foundations for an Agile law firm.

LPM does not have to be a complex or resource-heavy change for your firm to make. The basic tenets of LPM can be distilled down to a simple, universal set of best practices and rules that can and should be applied to every type of legal work and client. These can be built around the LPM framework with everyone in the firm educated as part of their core professional training on your firm's approach to running a legal matter effectively, founded on LPM best practice.

"It is important to remember that every lawyer who has had responsibility for a client matter has already been a project manager."

The goal is for your firm to embed this fundamental 'LPM 101' framework as a non-negotiable fundamental firm value and standard and, as soon as you feel ready, incorporate this cast-iron standard in your marketing, pitching and engagement terms with clients; something many competitors will still be unable to offer. The more complex application of LPM to larger, multi-faceted matters can be built on these basic foundations as a series of extensions and additional features and tools, making the universal firmwide LPM programme a fully integrated, coherent whole. Yet again, it is best to walk before you try to run and focus initially on the absolute universal basics of good Agile LPM.

As a minimum, these core standards should include:

- clearly defined, agreed and documented terms of engagement;
- how time, fees and costs will be managed;
- transparent scope of work and exclusions, related back to the agreed fee and how additional costs would relate to out-of-scope work;
- when and how the client will be updated on progress and costs;
- how any change request, affecting scope, timescale, costs or outcomes, will be notified, discussed and agreed;
- matter kick-off and post-matter debrief procedures; and
- simple matter plan with timeline and resources identified.

6. Implementing LPM – how do we get our people engaged with LPM training?

It is important to remember that every lawyer who has had responsibility for a client matter has already been a project manager. For those lawyers who have spent years, as they gain seniority and maybe partnership, taking responsibility for clients and matters, some form of matter/project management is unavoidable and essential to get the job done. The experienced lawyer, therefore, is almost certainly an 'accidental project manager'. Applying good project management is central to managing legal matters.

Experienced lawyers faced with the introduction of LPM into their firm or department will make the point that they have been practising and refining their skills in this area for decades. Bills get paid, transactions and cases successfully concluded, and clients come back again with their next matter. They are doing something *right*. Which can harden resistance to any new programme of LPM education.

To my mind, the very fact that there is such a large constituency of 'accidental project managers' underlines the case for investing in providing these lawyers with upgraded, updated and refreshed skills in such a critical area of their work. These days we are all always learning,

> *"Start small, pilot your programme and broadcast your successes."*

all of the time. Learning some new tools, tricks, techniques for managing the matters that form the basis of all of our work seems to make sense. Before rolling out LPM training I would use the following questions to turn sceptical lawyers into curious lawyers:

- Are you personally responsible for the delivery, budget, timeliness and client satisfaction of matters or phases within matters?
- Do you know about the latest, effective developments in project management best practice and how they can be applied to legal work?
- Have you adapted your matter management approach to ensure you are getting the best out of the data and technology now available to you?
- Are you clear what we tell clients about the firm's best practice guidelines and our commitments on matter management and client service?
- Where alternative fee arrangements apply, are you confident that you have all the tools to enable you to ensure the matter is managed in accordance with the fee?
- What techniques do you have for ensuring that changes to scope, timeline and potentially input/fees are understood and agreed by the client and not the source of later disagreement and write-off?

- Is the latest thinking among clients (especially corporate legal departments) about what constitutes good LPM understood and built into your approach to managing matters?
- Do you have to coordinate or manage the activity of multiple lawyers/staff on one matter? Are those lawyers located in different teams and locations?

You might also use compliance with your bar association's requirements to encourage engagement. In England and Wales, the Solicitors Regulation Authority (SRA) requires solicitors to demonstrate competence in core project management principles. Section D of the SRA's Solicitor Competence Statement[46] lists as essential competences tasks such as scoping, resource management, budget management, monitoring progress, communicating progress and managing project change. In the United States, John E Grant, founder of Agile Attorney Consulting, points out that the ABA Model Rules for Professional Conduct Rules 1.1–1.5 "have to do with competence, organisation, communication and managing resources, all of which are fundamental to project management. I argue that understanding basic project management concepts is required by the Ethics Rules".[47]

Your lawyers should also appreciate that using LPM tools and techniques will help them to operate within any Outside Counsel Guidelines (OCGs), which are an increasingly common and popular tactic for corporate legal to manage external legal outcomes and spend. Law firms can struggle with the complexity, prescriptiveness and volume of these guidelines but integrating these OCGs into your LPM methodology can help manage this issue.

As with any change programme, clearly explaining and then demonstrating the benefits (especially the 'what's in it for me') is going to be critical. That usually means running credible but initially small-scale, limited scope pilots and trials, with clear ROI and metrics. Proving the effectiveness of LPM in specific practices and teams is widely regarded as having been the most successful route by those who have led LPM initiatives. Start small, pilot your programme and broadcast your successes.

Most LPM practitioners inside firms would like to run more education and training to support their LPM programmes and often find it necessary to relaunch or refresh the LPM programme in order to get a better understanding and engagement embedded around their firm. LPMs have often found it tough to establish their credibility and capability with a sceptical, under-informed lawyer audience. Do not leave project managers unsupported in this area – provide plenty of endorsements, regular communication platforms and very public and sustained leadership sponsorship of these new roles.

Embracing and embedding LPM into the firm's core processes, values and client service standards can generate a substantial benefit to competitive position and work winning. Law firms are exploiting LPM to differentiate themselves from competitors. Perhaps the most celebrated example in recent years has been Seyfarth Shaw LLP, which has used a lean methodology to identify, manage and optimise key processes between itself and its clients, employing technology and specialised project managers to deliver them. Similarly, Clifford Chance has trained its lawyers on 'continuous improvement' techniques as part of a programme to model and improve processes with clients on specific transaction types.

Any major change that affects how most people in the firm do their work will have adversaries and blockers who resist the project. Ensure that you address this potential resistance by consulting, piloting and working with early adopters and enthusiasts, and explaining and overcoming fears. You need to be prepared for some initial knockbacks and understand the reasons for any initial resistance. You also need to ensure your advocates and allies help you drive the change forward; keeping them informed, engaged and involved in key decisions on direction and improvements. Using Agile principles here is critical – you need to be in a continuous learning loop, ready to test, iterate and redesign.

Agile first steps – client-centricity
- Ask all leaders, managers and partners to identify how they will deliver more value to clients over the next year.
- Collect, understand and use regular client satisfaction feedback, using a rigorous methodology (examples include NPS, CES, C-SAT) and IT tool.
- Set up recognition and reward mechanisms that exclusively target client-centred behaviour and improvements.
- Review and update your standards for LPM, using the ideas in this report.
- Pilot Agile LPM in one area of your firm.
- Introduce client journey mapping skills – start with your practice groups, marketing and IT functions.
- Trial using virtual or physical Kanban boards, including in a legal team, and share the learning gained.

III. Constantly innovating and improving

1. Introducing innovation

Our first Agile Attribute placed clients right at the centre of the Agile law firm. You know who we are focused on. This chapter turns its attention to what you need to do differently. As with most aspects of Agile this will require both a shift in mindset and a shift in behaviour across the firm. We know that the people in our organisations are prone to be uncomfortable with and wary about change. The VUCA world and the Agile model responding to it ask everyone to actively seek constant change; continuously searching for new learning, innovating and improving our services and products. The electric jolt of the COVID-19 pandemic and the waves of change that emanated out from it have driven home a lesson about the never-stable world we all now live in. Any residual assumption that 'some things will never change', lingering longer in the legal world than in many other sectors, has been replaced by 'change or die'.

This chapter looks at how this core Agile Attribute of constantly innovating and improving can be applied to law firms in both the design and development of new legal products and services and the constant, incremental improvement of our existing services. Both are valid and essential competencies for the Agile law firm. The school of thought that dismisses incremental improvement as tinkering at the edges while we should be disrupting has a good point when applied to law firms as a whole – they are wide open to disruption by new entrants, alternative providers and legal tech solutions. For an individual firm, though, continuous improvement of the client experience is absolutely essential; any Agile journey has to start here.

Innovation is regularly described to me as an overused word in the legal industry right now. It certainly is used a lot. And it sits firmly at the centre of the Agile law firm model and of this chapter. In my view, however, we can complain about overuse of the word when we have collectively got to grips with innovating in legal services; something we are a long way off.

There is a lingering perception around that word 'innovation' that it demands something akin to game-changing genius. That its outputs will be complex, hard-to-grasp and dramatically different. But your watchword for improving client services should instead be simplicity ("always simplify, don't complify" as Richard Hill, managing director at GL Law, reminded me when I spoke to him about this report). Keep things simple, capable of being delivered by your self-managed teams and start with the absolutely core features your client needs and values. Resist the temptation to just keep loading more features, bells, whistles and bows onto your service. Innovate and improve in short

"Lawyers and law firms have a lot to learn from the Agile methodologies which began in the software industry and have spread widely across industries."

bursts and then evaluate the impact, before moving onto the next features. Law firms should find this kind of discipline easier to handle than software businesses did when Agile first took hold – if we are honest we tend not to be addicted to constantly adding a long list of new features to our services. But even lawyers can get carried away based on initial successes or by a long list of potential improvements your client listening or innovation programme produces.

Lawyers and law firms have a lot to learn from the Agile methodologies which began in the software industry and have spread widely across industries. This chapter will attempt to explain how some of those lessons can be embedded into our world of clients, matters, filings and court forms. Legal services, however, are not software. We need to avoid the pitfalls of trying to replace one rigid, if sometimes haphazard and inconsistent, approach to delivering client value with another set of rules that still does not really fit the need.

So, this chapter focuses on how Agile and related methodologies used in other sectors can be, and have been, adapted for use in legal services. In particular, in improving legal service delivery to clients. That statement comes with another warning – be wary of a focus on internally driven innovation that too often generates changes that customers don't want or aren't willing to pay for. It is an easy trap to fall into, as getting under the skin of what your clients truly need is a time-consuming and sometimes uncomfortable job. It can feel so much easier to, instead, respond to what your lawyers and partners want to see happen.

> **Agile toolkit – Agile product development and project management**
> The Agile methodology is founded on a process view of human collaboration. It has been primarily used in software, website, technology, creative and marketing industries. The Agile approach contrasts sharply with the traditional, Waterfall, approach, as I outlined in the first chapter. In the Agile product development approach, the project is seen as a series of relatively small tasks conceived and executed as the situation demands in an adaptive manner, rather than as a completely pre-planned and sequential process. It involves frequent testing of the project under development. It is the only technique in which the client is actively involved.
>
> I am not going to use a lot of the space in this report unpicking the core Agile methods used in software and other industries. Many of the other related tools and approaches featured in more detail in this and other chapters have been adapted and adopted more successfully by lawyers. However, it is worth being familiar with the

fundamentals of the Agile product and project management method and some of its key terms.

In the Agile method, work should be done in small, autonomous, cross-functional teams working in short cycles (sprints). These sprints are planned to address relatively small, manageable tasks and deliver a working solution ready for testing. These tasks are referred to as user stories (or sometimes customer or client stories). That is an important piece of terminology – rather than talk about 'features', 'functions' or 'fixes' the Agile approach emphasises the human and client-centric. These are stories that describe what it is the end user or client wants to do or achieve, not just a request for a piece of code to be written. Or, in legal terms, a document to be drafted.

Agile techniques are applied to big product and software development programmes. But the emphasis of Agile, as you will have grasped by now, is to have small teams working on bite-sized challenges. Agile is therefore built around a break-down of very big challenges to the user story and task level. I won't try to explain the whole breakdown structure but the following terms are used for the various levels:

- *Product roadmap:* a plan of action for how a product or solution will evolve over time. The product roadmap is expressed and visualised as a set of initiatives plotted along a timeline;
- *Theme:* an organisational goal around which initiatives are created;
- *Epic:* a large body of work with one overall objective (part of an initiative) – what might have been a project in traditional approaches; and
- *User story:* a task that reflects a specific user requirement. The tasks and sprints that address user stories are prioritised according to end user/client value.

The aim of the Agile development approach is to rapidly get to a point where a minimum viable product (MVP) can be tested, ideally by the end user. This enables the continuous feedback loop from the ultimate client or end user and allows solutions to be iterated rapidly and regularly.

Agile toolkit – design thinking
I expect most readers will have heard of design thinking. It is another example of a mindset and approach that was born in and propagated by industries very different from legal services, but which has been adapted and embraced by organisations in the legal

"Design thinking is a multi-disciplinary, highly collaborative model for designing – and redesigning – and improving products, services, processes, indeed entire organisations."

world in recent years. So much so, in fact, that there is a recognised 'legal design' movement. Rather like other 'legal' appellations, including legal project management, there is little truly unique about the application of the original ideas to the law, but it seems to be more comfortable and attractive for a wary legal audience to believe something has been specifically developed for lawyers.

Design thinking is a multi-disciplinary, highly collaborative model for designing – and redesigning – and improving products, services, processes, indeed entire organisations. It is inherently Agile and has been used most famously in product design and development and, like Agile itself, sits at the heart of many of the 21st century's most successful companies. The results of many studies by business academics have reinforced a conclusion that design-led companies outperform other companies.

That word 'design' rightly suggests creative thinking is to the fore, but design thinking is also founded on analysis and rigorous discovery. As it has been applied to more mainstream business processes, products and problems across multiple industries, the initial business wariness of using such an inherently creative, often colourful and visual, toolkit has subsided.

design growth/change mindset

Start with end in mind – what does client want?

As readers will expect by now, design thinking puts the client or customer at the heart of the design experience, treating them as human beings with problems. Design thinking is a mindset as much as a discipline. It means starting with the end user and working backwards. When we start with the issues, requirements and needs of legal clients, we find that addressing many of their issues represents more of a design challenge than a legal challenge.

The name most closely identified with design thinking is IDEO, the global design company famous for creating the iconic first Apple mouse. IDEO have popularised and productised the design thinking process, emphasising three essential ingredients for great design: empathy, ideation and experimentation.

Empathy is an undervalued and often misunderstood concept that runs throughout this report and requires you to be focused on truly understanding your clients' needs, perspectives and lives. An unquenchable sense of curiosity powers empathy. Listening is probably the core skill used – getting more of your people engaged in design thinking exercises will improve their listening and then understanding and your clients will be happy about that.

"When we start with the issues, requirements and needs of legal clients, we find that addressing many of their issues represents more of a design challenge than a legal challenge."

Ideation involves the open, unbounded and high-volume generation of ideas, tapping into experiences and inputs from wide and diverse sources, especially the multi-skilled team developing the design. Successful ideation is built on seven rules IDEO has laid out[48]:

- *defer judgement;*
- *encourage wild ideas;*
- *build on the ideas of others;*
- *stay focused on the topic;*
- *participate in one conversation at a time;* 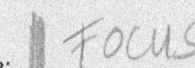 FOCUS
- *be visual; and*
- *go for quantity.*

Experimentation is based on the scientific model of identifying and then testing hypotheses and being ready to fail, revise and restart the test and restate the hypothesis. The emphasis on experimentation and an objective, bias-free approach to testing is critical here. Multiple ideas should be produced and progressed. The process does not restrict, edit or short-circuit choosing the best idea, as we are tempted to do in real-world work situations. IDEO have encouraged the whole world to *embrace ambiguity*; avoid leaping to conclusions and be willing to forego familiarity and certainty for the risk and associated with exploring new ideas. Do not set out on a mission to design or redesign a client-facing product, service or process until you have taken the time to apply your empathy and gain a genuine understanding of them.

There are five phases of design thinking (see overleaf) and the basic model for 'how to do it' follows these, with regular flow back from one phase to the previous one, as iteration and experimentation are so key to the process. There are plenty of different ways of running a design thinking project but they tend to focus around a workshop where a multi-disciplined group work together through the phases. Post-it notes and walls feature heavily! The workshops should be fun and highly creative. But there should also be enough seriousness, genuine output and return to ensure lawyers don't dismiss this as some kind of game that squanders potential billable hours.

The COVID pandemic disrupted this default approach as it did so much else. It seems unlikely in these post-COVID years that you can expect to get a multi-disciplinary team to gather physically every time, still less if you want to pull in people from multiple locations or from clients. The default model will probably shift to remote Zoom and Teams sessions, probably shorter or punctuated by more downtime, and breaks, using electronic tools, screen-sharing and virtual breakout rooms.

- *Empathise* – team members observe, listen, explore their clients' lives and world and understand their behaviour and perspective around the legal service you are examining. As I have already pointed out, design thinking – and Agile in general – is human-centred and this phase is critical to establish the client as a person and position the challenge we are addressing within the context of their lives. Without taking the time required to empathise in the first phase, our attempts to frame the problem in the next phase will suffer from a whole litany of our own assumptions, perceptions and biases and, sadly, often a pitifully limited understanding of our clients' actual experience. I know that many people in law firms will need to see tangible, compelling evidence that this investment of time and emotional energy is worth the return. But that is something that can only be tested by seriously applying the model, and the empathise phase especially, as you trial it in your own firm. Although 'empathise' appears here as a *phase*, you should continue to utilise empathy throughout your projects.
- *Define* – team members consolidate their learning from the first phase, creating packages of insights that help define the problem. This may involve building a map of the client journey, showing how clients experience your service, and identifying their critical touchpoints and interactions. Using the core Agile methodologies, these insights can be packaged into *user or client stories*.
- *Ideate* – team members are encouraged to contribute as many ideas and questions as they can, remaining open-minded and imaginative. Team members do work both alone and collaboratively throughout this phase, developing each other's ideas, using 'yes and' thinking. The focus is on generating as many ideas as possible initially – *diverging*. Only when that is done then *converging* into a small, preferred set of ideas. The output will often be stated as a 'How might we...?' question, which turns around a negative problem into a positive prospective solution (eg, How might we make it easier for our clients to review and sign documents related to their case in less time and on multiple devices?).
- *Prototype* – teams develop tools and models that bring their ideas, often still more than one, to life. These can be simple mock-up test applications, charts, stories or storyboards, video or even physical models. These will not be polished or ready to release; speed and spontaneity are key, as is the willingness to iterate and rebuild the prototypes multiple times if necessary – something that is undermined by having perfect prototypes that have taken a lot of time and effort to create.
- *Test* – teams engage with clients or users to test the

prototype. During this experimentation phase, you are not just looking for clients' formal feedback but for less conscious reactions, perceptions, emotions. As at previous stages, you are still not using a production quality model; the minimum viable product concept comes into play – how quickly and easily can you produce something you can meaningfully test. Teams need to be ready to fail, learn and rebuild. As with prototyping, testing is still an iterative process that allows the team to refine and hone their solution.

Unlike some big changes, you really can get started quickly and easily with design thinking, without needing to make a big hullabaloo or generate stratospheric expectations (or objections!). It is established practice when driving change in difficult environments to begin in one area, team or problem and that will certainly work well here.

You do need to build some knowledge and skills before you strike out though. Before introducing design thinking, look at options for getting some training for whoever is going to be involved in the initial project(s). There are now plenty of online, virtual courses and webinars, both cross-industry (including those run by IDEO themselves) and tailored to legal. You may well be able to get involved in a real-life design sprint or jam along with other firms, creating real-life solutions at the same time as you learn the process. As back up, having a consultant or someone on hand who has successfully run design thinking exercises makes a lot of sense, until your internal champions feel confident and have more experience.

You will need sponsors throughout your organisation who will support, champion and guide the people with the ideas – your *intrapreneurs*. Without this advocacy and assistance, there is a high risk that the firm will reject many of the attempts to introduce change and improvement and fail to progress to a more Agile state. Identify these people and give them your unambiguous backing, and the opportunity to learn and develop their skills as innovation sponsors.

Firms who are a little further down the line or have a strong case for investment, could look to bring in service design experience from outside the firm, and maybe outside the profession, on a more regular or permanent hire basis. Many larger firms have hired in innovation professionals and created innovation and design teams, as I will outline later in this report. But stimulating the use and sharing of design thinking skills from the bottom-up is at least as important in my view. I do not believe we want to see law firms with a bigger but very separate cadre of innovation and transformation professionals who have entirely different mindsets, skills and priorities from the lawyer population. We have to develop these skills in all of our people, not just a small elite.

Getting started on internal processes and improvements may seem like a strange suggestion, when so much of the powerful value of using design thinking rests in the impact it can have directly on client touchpoints. But there is a case for limbering up and honing some skills in this area, where there are plenty of problems looking for solutions and you can build experience and celebrate successes before tackling anything with clients 'in the room'.

In conclusion, I'd recommend getting started with design thinking in one or two places around your firm right now. The initial gathering of skills and knowledge for a small pioneer group won't take long or cost much. Your mindset should be that design thinking skills are going to be a core component of essential competencies for your future firm and planning how to embed them should start as soon as possible. One of the great things about this approach is that so much of it can be learned by doing.

Design thinking in the legal world
The escalating influence of design thinking methods in the legal sector has been one of the most dramatic examples of the law's assimilation of Agile working. It is not too hard to work out why, despite the potential lawyer aversion to something that sounds like it belongs in the world of hip furniture and mood-boards. The very clear client-centric focus strikes a chord with many lawyers. While design thinking does employ an alien terminology – words like 'ideation', 'iteration' and 'empathy' can easily turn people off – this language is warmer and more human than the mechanistic language of techniques derived from manufacturing and engineering factory floors. Legal design converts, I suspect, are also attracted to feeling plugged into the same worldwide innovation community as those smart design folks at the likes of Apple, Spotify and Amazon. Finally, the timing of these design ideas arriving in legal is perfect – just as lawyers in all kinds of settings are grappling with the opportunities and challenges of increasingly common legal tech and as the productisation and digitisation of legal services, especially post-COVID, are top of our agenda.

Design thinking can support law firms in multiple areas of their work. It is being deployed extensively to design and develop new products and services, including those based around legal tech. This is one important way in which a shared set of new ideas, approaches and skills are being transmitted back and forth between the ALSP, legal tech and law firm worlds.

"Firms are also applying design thinking approaches directly to redesigning and innovating their existing processes and client service delivery routines – what is sometimes called 'legal process improvement'."

Firms are also applying design thinking approaches directly to redesigning and innovating their existing processes and client service delivery routines – what is sometimes called 'legal process improvement'. The watchwords in these process design exercises have shifted a little. Where the focus has often been more internal, with design focused on automation, streamlining and efficiency, the focus has shifted, adding to those still viable objectives, the goal of creating a frictionless, effortless, intuitive service experience for your clients. How easy it is to do business with you is a key measure of design success.

Josh Kubicki uses the term *business design* and has done a lot of work on how this can be adopted in the law firm setting, not least during his years as one of the innovation leads at Seyfarth Shaw. Josh is now co-founder and Design Lead at radical legal design house Bold Duck Studios. He describes business design as: "The conversion of a customer problem into sustainable value for the customer and our business. It is a human-centred approach to innovation. It applies the principles and practices of design to help organizations create new value and new forms of competitive advantage."[49]

The rising popularity of design thinking in law is evidenced by the regularity with which we now see activities and events badged as Design Sprints, Hackathons and Design Jams. These are being run as part of big global programmes such as Law Without Walls, the very influential baby of Michelle DeStefano, Professor at Miami Law School. They are also popping up around the world led by academic organisations, by legal tech providers, by regional or sectoral collaborative organisations and, internally, by law firm innovation heads and departments, who are now running annual competitions and festivals of innovation. The widespread use of that word 'innovation' across the legal sector in recent years often refers to activity that is informed by design thinking.

Stanford Legal Design Lab is an interdisciplinary team at Stanford Law School & Design School ('d.school'), working at the intersection of human-centred design, technology and law to build a new generation of legal products and services. The Lab was founded and is run by Margaret Hagan, one of the best-known legal designers, and their research is particularly focused on new initiatives to make the civil justice system more equitable and accessible. A recent success involved developing and launching eviction legal help tools in the immediate aftermath of the COVID-19 pandemic. The Stanford team have developed and then shared new models of user-friendly, accessible, and engaging legal services. Margaret's book on legal design, *Law By Design*, is available as a free download and is a great, short read on this subject.[50]

Over at Vanderbilt Law School, another US pioneer and champion of design thinking in the law, Cat Moon, has developed a course on human-centred design called "Legal Problem Solving".[51] Underlining Cat's work is an emphasis on curiosity as a 'super-power'. It is great to see young lawyers-to-be getting trained early in their career on using design thinking as a problem-solving tool and developing an Agile mindset to complement the legal skills they are learning.

Agile toolkit – user or client experience (UX/CX)

Design thinking addresses all of the interactions, channels and touchpoints across the organisation and the client base. It is a wide-screen, multi-disciplinary approach to design and redesign. I now want to drill down a little and highlight two closely related design concepts: *customer or client experience* (CX) and *user experience* (UX).

Customer experience (CX) is a broader concept than UX. It covers the client or customer's experiences with all channels and products. Mapping the full client lifecycle over multiple services and years can be a start-point for CX redesign.

User experience (UX) is product or service-specific. It has become well-known and an object of fascination as it relates to dominant consumer products from the likes of Apple and Samsung, services like Uber or retail brands like McDonalds or Starbucks (although note that in most of those cases there is also a lot of investment in relationship-focused CX too). It refers to the user's experience with the usability and interface design of a specific product or service.

These concepts can be applied to the design and improvement of legal services. They are a more granular aspect of broader design thinking. There has been some excellent work on both UX and CX in relation to legal services, especially as they have become more digitised. Here is a checklist of the features of good client experience, based on some work done by Jordan Furlong, which is an excellent start-point for you to measure how your main client services perform[52]:

- *Response* – first time, on time.
- *Delivery* – what is asked for and agreed on is what gets delivered, as specified.
- *Transparency* – fees billed promptly and clearly, with no surprises.
- *Value* – work is priced clearly and the value and justification explained.
- *Accessible* – clients can get hold of information about their matter when they want it and get an answer from the firm when they need one.
- *Responsible* – there is a primary single point of contact who is identified and actually available.
- *Consistent* – no matter which part of the firm or person the client deals with, the experience is similarly excellent.
- *Personal* – the client receives a strong feeling of being known, understood and personally important to the firm and the people they deal with.
- *Predictable* – no unpleasant surprises in terms of outcomes or timing.
- *Enhanced* – benefits, knowledge, features and support that the client doesn't have to ask for or pay extra for, and demonstrate the firm's capability and care.

2. Lean and Six Sigma
Lean and Six Sigma are methodologies that have had a wide impact on business management over decades. They are closely related and often used in tandem (as Lean Six Sigma) to address a process problem. They are both used to tackle inefficiency and waste, though Lean is more of a set of principles, whereas Six Sigma is a more

developed problem-solving methodology. There are many passionate and well-entrenched advocates of one over the other out there and there is always some controversy flaring up about the relative merits of the two approaches.

There is a cultural generalisation, generated in large part by the types of business that have championed each approach and how they have applied them, that personifies the Six Sigma approach as more remote, controlling and harsh (in its effect on people/the workforce) and Lean as more open, democratic and inclusive.

Law firm and corporate legal department pathfinders in process improvement have often chosen to borrow substantial elements from Lean and Six Sigma but have adapted these tools to the professional services environment. Most decided against attempting a 'pure' implementation of either (or both) of these approaches. There are some companies and individuals in the legal world who have been refining Lean and Six Sigma tools for use by lawyers for some time. One of the trailblazers in this area is Catherine Alman MacDonagh, the co-founder of the Legal Lean Sigma Institute (LLSI).[53] Since 2011, LLSI has been creating and delivering courses, alongside consulting assignments, to teach the application of Lean, Six Sigma and other process improvement methodologies in law. Their certification courses are designed specifically for the legal profession and LLSI's Yellow Belt Certification courses are offered at Suffolk Law School and at George Washington University.

Legal Lean Sigma Design™ combines elements of design thinking, Lean Sigma and project management methodologies and tools. That synthesis demonstrates one of the core precepts of this report – there are a range of good Agile tools and the most effective elements of them can be combined and adapted to the legal environment. I particularly like their emphasis on integrating project management – how you *manage* the process – with the process and service design tools. Catherine Alman MacDonagh also regularly makes the excellent point that too many organisations are rushing to add technology to a process that has yet to be improved.

> **Agile toolkit – Lean in a nutshell**
> Lean is one of the many business management tools and ideas still in widespread use that emerged from the Toyota Production System in the last century. The focus is on breaking down processes to the bare bone essentials, hence the name 'Lean'. Lean aims to separate out waste from value in processes and eliminate the waste and 'non-value-added'. Successful Lean projects will help you "do the right things".

Practitioners usually feel that Lean is more suitable and easily assimilated by lawyers than Six Sigma. The concept of reducing lead or process time is well understood as clients demand results faster. The idea of 'non-value-added' activity also resonates with busy lawyers who know that some of their time (and many lawyers might say 'most' of their time) is taken up with 'admin', 'bureaucracy', 'compliance', 'form filling' and a host of less pleasant terms. In fact, if Lean did not exist it seems likely that, right now, lawyers would have to invent it!

The following Lean ideas can be, and have been, used to improve processes and products in legal, often synthesised with other approaches such as design thinking:

Process lead (or cycle) time – at the heart of Lean is the concept of the time it takes to move through the entire process from input (eg, a client's accident claim being referred) to output (eg, the claim being settled and case closed). The aim of Lean process improvement is to reduce this time and in particular attack non-value-added activity, reducing the time and cost of the process.

Process cycle efficiency (PCE) – a metric that measures overall process health. It is calculated by dividing value-add time in the process by total process lead time. A higher PCE shows a healthier process, of course, as a higher per cent of total lead time is spent on value-added activities (see the next point below). The lower PCE per cent processes are those with the most potential opportunities for efficiencies and cost savings. It is not unusual to find pre-improvement PCE values of less than 10%.

Non-value-add analysis – a particularly valuable additional step in applying Lean to the legal sector is the identification of value-add and non-value-add process steps. The aim is then to minimise or eliminate the non-value-add steps as part of the process improvement effort. In this context 'value-add' refers to activity that is essential to deliver a service to the client, the client would be willing and happy to pay for or would complain about if you stopped doing it. Law firms shouldn't equate 'value-add' precisely with 'chargeable activity', but there is obviously some correlation. Some activity is business non-value-added (BNVA) – while not required by the client, it is required by the firm itself in order to support value-added activity.

Examples (by no means an exhaustive list) of non-value-added activity found in many types of process and certainly relevant to law firms include:

- excessive handling of information and documents beyond what is essential to move from one value-added activity to the next;
- rework required to fix errors;
- unnecessary authorisations, supervision or checking (based on adopting a 'get it right first time' mentality);
- waiting for prior steps to complete or information to be input/delivered/sent;
- delay;
- overelaboration of advice or documents – exceeding client requirements and demands;
- excessive resourcing of tasks or meetings;
- unnecessary printing, filing, distribution and other handling of paper; and
- multiple data entry steps.

The reduction of non-value-added activity can obviously reduce process cost but, by reducing complexity can also reduce errors and, by reducing lead time, can improve client satisfaction.

Agile toolkit – Six Sigma in a nutshell

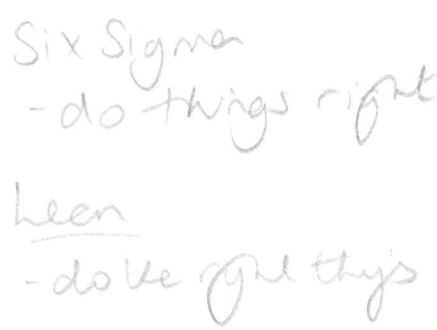

Six Sigma is probably the world's best-known process improvement tool and its fame has even penetrated the legal profession. It does sound a bit like a secret society but is in fact a series of disciplined business practices designed to improve processes and, in particular, to eliminate defects. Six Sigma's purpose is "do things right" (contrast with Lean: "do the right things").

The methodology was first formulated by Bill Smith at Motorola in 1986. It borrows martial arts ranking terminology – accredited practitioners are awarded coloured 'belts'. 'Sigma' is a statistical term that measures how far a given process deviates from perfection. The central idea behind Six Sigma is that if you can measure how many 'defects' you have in a process, you can systematically eliminate them and dramatically improve quality and business performance. A Six Sigma defect is defined as anything outside of customer specifications, and to achieve Six Sigma Quality, a process must produce no more than 3.4 defects per million.

The focus is therefore firmly on eliminating defects and maximising highly repeatable quality. As a result, there is an understandable assumption that it is only suitable for manufacturing-based organisations. However, multiple variations on Six Sigma have been produced that adapt it to service industries – see *Lean Six Sigma for Service* by one of the foremost thinkers and authors on Six Sigma, Michael L George.[54]

The main underlying structure for identifying the root causes of process inefficiencies and issues and implementing a successful solution is referred to as DMAIC (Define – Measure – Analyse – Improve – Control). This model is usable in a multitude of different scenarios, in lawyer's offices as well as in large corporates.

The advantage of DMAIC is that it provides a simple and very logical approach to process improvement. Unlike many of the most Agile methods, Six Sigma and DMAIC are designed to be followed sequentially and there is not the same emphasis on looping backwards to previous stages, iteration or testing. But the elimination of defects, quality issues and inefficiency is still a fundamental goal to delivering more Agile, consistent and excellent client service. You will also see the connection between the Six Sigma model and other Agile tools – an emphasis on a thorough define stage upfront, extensive use of objective data and eradication of assumption, perception and bias, and the concept of continuous improvement baked-in.

Agile first steps – constantly innovating and improving
- Evaluate how well innovation is being stimulated and delivered in your firm.
- Introduce the Agile product and project methodology into your product and service development and major change project work.
- Inject design thinking knowledge and skill into your core learning and development programmes, emphasising empathy and ideation.
- Use the Lean and Six Sigma in a nutshell section to evaluate your approach to eliminating waste, non-value-adding effort and defects across the firm – how can you improve your results?
- Ensure that your performance management process enshrines innovation and improvement objectives and development goals for teams and individuals across the firm.

IV. Insight-driven

1. Velocity
Velocity is now a critical success factor for law firms. Readers from parts of the business world, including many law firm clients, might do a double-take at that sentence. Perhaps because they simply do not associate moving quickly or pursuing change at pace with the legal profession. Perhaps because the relationship between speed and business success is such a self-evident feature of their environment that it is hard to believe that isn't the case for every industry.

In an Agile world, there is an emphasis on responding and pivoting at speed to external and internal stimuli. But Agile organisations do not simply react, using gut instinct, to events. They develop well-honed and scientific processes that continuously create insights. This allows them to also *anticipate* and predict the impact of forces in the future.

How do you increase the tempo of an entire organisation? That sounds particularly challenging where speed has not traditionally been valued highly – lawyers as a profession have often actively resisted, where they could, the encroaching and ever-increasing pace of modern business. In law there is an undercurrent that faster is often riskier.

The best Agile organisations, including many of the greatest success stories of the 21st century, have founded their success on a super-evolved capability to respond to and anticipate changes in their customer base, market environment, technology and society. They have had to explode the bureaucracy model, where time is wasted while work lies in queues, awaiting approvals. They need to support this capability with an organisation-wide ability to make business decisions much faster. Agile firms need to *rapidly convert information into insight into business impact.*

To achieve that level, decision making needs to be distributed, not rigidly centralised. Agile self-managed teams, especially those directly serving the client, need a constant flow of information and, more critically, insight. But they also need the skills to interpret and then act on it. Decision rights cannot be hazy or undocumented, open to dispute or misinterpretation. Nor can they be attached blindly to status or reserved to a small pool of senior, central management. Time to act is slowed right down in these circumstances and decisions are made a long way from the client. Sometimes access to business-critical information and insight is reserved for a small group of high-status individuals who are typically over-busy and receive far too many reports. Senior leaders may not be trained or skilled in rapid interpretation of business information and may be juggling client-facing workloads that lead to internal information being de-prioritised. Yes, I have just described almost every law firm. Few law firm management teams have managed to apply to business management the same professional and intellectual ability to collate, understand, interpret and act on information, often at speed, used daily in their legal work. Law firms, on the whole, are not insight-driven organisations.

The flow, cadence and accountability of business decisions in any organisation is one of the most critical factors in its success. Yet it is seldom seriously analysed as a critical business process, alongside the more obvious transactional workflows. I will now examine that process – how you translate data into information to then create insights and, ultimately, deliver business change and an outcome or impact that creates value to clients and to the firm. I call this the information/insight/impact model. Two burning questions for law firms today are how well this process works and how quickly it moves.

2. The insight-driven firm

Becoming truly insight-driven is a benchmark for any Agile organisation. That underlying agility is facilitated and enhanced by the rapid cycling of data, information and insights into decision and action. The outcome of becoming insight-driven is real business impact – competitive advantage, time-to-market, continuous improvement across all aspects of the firm.

"Agile self-managed teams, especially those directly serving the client, need a constant flow of information and, more critically, insight."

Specifically, Agile organisations shift insight-driven decision making from an executive-level pursuit into an all-employee pursuit. Small self-managed teams require the access to transparent, real-time and high-quality information that firm leadership once saw as its sole preserve.

Agile firms need forward-looking insights, not just historical results. This is now almost conventional wisdom – use information to map the road ahead and do not spend all your management time and energy looking in the rear-view mirror. Take a look at the apparently most important management information served up in your firm – does it adhere to that principle?

A professional service variation on an insight-driven organisation (or IDO) puts a structured decision-making *process* at the heart of the firm. The ubiquity and value of insight to the modern Agile organisation demands that analytics capabilities are embedded right across it. This is another component of the Agile principle of building multi-disciplinary teams. Firms should be focused on building insight delivery into everything – business processes, workflows, application roll-outs and meeting agendas. Don't be shy about looking to shift the culture of the firm, it should embrace the importance of being data insight-driven. That process will be in operation not just monthly or quarterly (or, worse, annually – just when budgets and year-end come around), but daily, constantly. The firm embeds analysis and creation of insights from data and intelligence into structures, processes, reporting and performance management.

The first critical shift when becoming insight-driven is to reorient analysis and business intelligence activity from a focus on historical reporting to forward-looking insights. Rethink your current reporting, management information, performance management and information systems to turn 'dead-end' delivery of information that has no clear call-to-action or business outcome into a flow of insights that always triggers deeper investigation, decisions and actions at all levels of the firm.

The second shift is just as important. Firms have to search out, challenge and address the easy, habitual reliance on intuition, gut-feel, 'experience' or narrow strands of data. The way in which partners and managers in law firms use information and make decisions often follows the tendency in the wider world, prevalent on social media, to create 'echo chambers' where individuals only ever hear the views and information they expect and agree with. Consider how your partners approach information about their team, practice, office and you might

> *"The way in which partners and managers in law firms use information and make decisions often follows the tendency in the wider world, prevalent on social media, to create 'echo chambers' where individuals only ever hear the views and information they expect and agree with."*

see some parallels. Pushing an insight-driven culture across your firm involves challenging that instinctive reversion to individual assumption and bias.

3. Is data your 'new oil'?
Today's business world is inundated with terminology to which ever-greater importance is being attached: 'big data'; 'artificial intelligence'; 'digital transformation'; 'moneyball'; 'marginal gains'; 'predictive analytics'; 'data visualisation'; 'cyber security'; 'spend analysis'; 'smart contracts'; business intelligence'; and 'data science'. Business intelligence focuses primarily on analysing historical business data, whereas data science aims to make predictions about future performance. Each of these ideas is built on the critical importance of data to the 21st-century organisation.

Business intelligence (BI) is also a category of software that helps the business decision-making process by speeding up and improving the ingestion and analysis of large amounts of data in order to support those business decisions. BI software can yield outputs ranging from enhanced reports to predictive analysis, visualisation and scenario comparison. Until recently, an investment in BI technology would be very expensive, involving creation of a 'data warehouse' of data pulled from various systems which would then be mined to generate outputs. Many of these big BI tools were outside the reach of law firms but the emergence of flexible, often cloud 'as a service' BI systems, some of them tailored specifically to professionals, has transformed this picture in the last decade. Tellingly, the buzz term for BI was once decision support systems – a label that really describes how the outputs should be used.

Data is a valuable asset for every type of business, including law. Data is, in one memorable and much-used phrase, 'the new oil'. In a competitive market, maximising your ability to reveal insights hidden within your management information (MI) and client data is strategically essential to remaining Agile. 'Big data' is a phrase coined in the 1990s but really popularised around 2012. It refers to the explosion of data that is stored, searched and consumed in the post-internet world. Fuelled by the activities of Google, Facebook, Twitter and the democratisation of content creation, big data was also a result of the massive intensification of data collection by retailers, government and other agencies. The ability to process this exponential growth in data has only been possible through the development of tools based around the HADOOP programming framework.

This shift to a greater appreciation of the value of data and, ultimately, insight in legal businesses is in part a response to trends in the wider economy and society and in part an overdue challenge to the instinctive aversion to data-driven decisions that characterised law firms. For a profession that places huge value on evidence and knowledge in the context of work for clients but precious little on hard data and information that relates to the performance of the firm, this represents a big shift.

Perhaps the most immediate external factor pushing law firms to smarten up their act on analytics and business intelligence in the last few years has been, inevitably, client behaviour. The adoption of eBilling as a standard practice by large corporations in North America has triggered a chain reaction of action and counter-action taken by large law firms and their clients. The combined impact of the emergence of alternative fee arrangements (AFAs) and introduction of eBilling include:

- significant increase in electronic time, fee and billing data created and exchanged with clients;
- routine automated analysis of law firm billing data by corporate clients;
- increasing firm-to-firm comparison and fee benchmarking by corporate clients as eBilling systems evolve into legal spend management systems;
- AFA pricing requiring more sophisticated analysis (by both parties) of historic matters, predicted scenarios and variations/re-forecasts;
- adoption by law firms of matter analysis, planning and pricing software;
- shifting finance and performance management focus from fees and time only to profitability, as AFAs and changing commercial environment introduce new complexity;
- introduction and rapid growth of client-side corporate legal operations roles; and
- parallel introduction and growth of firm-side pricing, analytics and LPM directors.

Taken in total, and especially among the larger firm tier, these changes represent a very different environment in which information about fees, pricing and profitability is being assessed. Demand for more analysis and insight has increased from partners, practice heads, finance managers and firm leaders – as well, of course, as from the ultimate clients. Speed of response is more important than ever, especially where clients have pressed for very regular or near real-time updates on progress and fees. And a new layer of information professionals within both corporate legal departments and law firms are introducing previously unknown levels of information sophistication, in a behind the scenes 'cold war' race to understand the commercial performance and potential of legal work.

"Today, most law firms remain 'data rich but insight poor', impeding their efforts to create an Agile, insight-driven organisation."

[Handwritten note: What can we do to get more use out of our data?]

Agile toolkit – the information/insight/impact model

Today, most law firms remain 'data rich but insight poor', impeding their efforts to create an Agile, insight-driven organisation. The following will introduce some solutions for addressing that insight gap.

The primary objective is to introduce a rigorous approach to harnessing your data and creating insights that then support faster, better informed and actionable business decisions. Law firms do face some challenges that derive partly from the partnership model and how that dictates reporting, reward, remuneration and performance management structures. The pervading spirit of partner and practice autonomy can also obscure how well the data, insights and decision process is functioning. In some firms, few big business decisions are made at practice and team level from the point business plans and budgets are set through to the year end. 'Getting on with the job'
and 'gut instinct' can be valued more than making decisions based on data, empirical insight or trend analysis.

There are plenty of systems and tools in use, especially in Agile organisations, that can help improve that process. None reflect the *specific* context of the law firm and some years ago I developed a

[Handwritten note: need - faster better informed actionable business decisions]

more tailored model for law firm leaders that synthesised best practices in analytics and decision making. This information/insight/impact (i3) model is, in fact, a cycle rather than a linear process – the outputs (*impacts*) should continuously feed the firm's decision about *information* and data the firm looks to create, store, curate and publish.

Law firm management can utilise the model to achieve better-informed decision making and execution. This process should be a central part of any firm's management system. The i3 model deliberately takes some of the over-emphasis on the technology component of managing, storing and analysing data and instead places it on outcomes – generating new insight about performance and acting on this to make decisions and create business impact. This final stage – without which you will simply not get the return on your investment – is often ignored when the focus is on data management and the impetus and responsibility sits with IT or BI functions, rather than the firm's overall leadership.

The model has five distinct stages that enable firms to manage, improve and accelerate the process of converting data into measurable business impact, in the form of improved performance – including client service delivery. It is often deployed initially to introduce more structure and rigour to core commercial decisions around fees, pricing, resourcing and profitability at firm, practice, team, client and matter level.

This section takes you on a tour through the i3 model. As noted above, it is a cycle – ideally your firm will first think about impact – the business performance objectives and outcomes you are looking for, before then evaluating what information you require and whether the firm has the right data available. You will also note that another label – incentivisation – sits across all stages, end-to-end. The impact of incentives, reward, performance management and remuneration systems in law firms can have a significant impact on, and sometimes be a significant obstacle to, implementing successful information/insight/impact.

Figure 2. The components of incentivisation

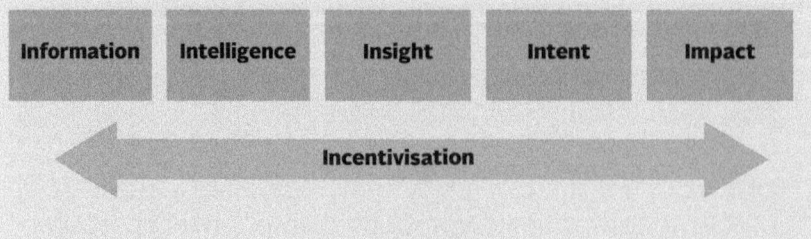

Stage 1: information

How do data and information differ? I have referred to data a lot, as I explained the explosion in volume, velocity and variety of data making up the emergence of big data. Information features as the initial stage of the i3 model, however, because it is more commonly what leaders and users of systems in law firms first encounter. Data is raw, unprocessed. It can refer to words, pictures, numbers, video, characters or sound, but it is not necessarily understandable if presented in this raw form. To become meaningful information, data has to be processed. Context is added and the information is in a form that can be understood and absorbed.

In common with any business change, implementing best practices around analytics and insight-driven decisions begins with agreeing objectives. Your i3 goals should be fully aligned with your business strategy and plans. Indeed, I generally recommend that firms incorporate the i3 model into their regular annual business planning cycle, reviewing the full model as you begin to establish high-level goals but before you drill down into the detail of budgeting. The more precise your firm can be about what improvement you are seeking in which dimensions, the more valuable and relevant the information/insight/impact process can be. In an Agile law firm, many of these improvements will relate directly to client service and experience – innovating to improve revenues and profitability, reducing unnecessary time and costs – but they can cover any part of your business.

Another information need which firms should reflect on at this stage is the increasing demand from corporate clients for their private practice firms to provide large volumes of detailed data and report to them. This can often be on a real-time and very regular basis. This demand – fuelled by the rise of corporate legal operations within in-house legal functions and especially extensive in data-centric industries such as insurance – is hard to refuse and is already also driving firms to develop their own analytics capability and software.

The i3 model can be used at firm, practice group, team, client or matter level. Or for an office, country, region or sector. Most of the examples given are for the entire firm, but you can kick-off using the model in a part of the firm to pilot new ways of thinking and working, or zone in on a specific business objective, perhaps where there is insufficient movement or achievement (eg, if profitability is proving stubbornly difficult to increase or growth in specific markets is slowing).

Step 1 – Consolidate your short-term business plan targets and medium/long-term strategic objectives. Include any required improvement in a financial/commercial dimension (including sales/fees, profitability, working capital, utilisation etc). Don't forget the client perspective – a good number of your objectives should relate to how you will meet client demands and retain/develop/grow client relationships, not just to how much you will extract from them in fees and profits.

Step 2 – Ensure the objectives identified in step 1 are measurable and identify what measure(s) should be used. Use the standard SMART acronym to test whether they are well-defined – objectives should be Stretching, Measurable, Agreed, Realistic, Timed.

Step 3 – For each objective and measure identified in Step 2 determine how *often* you should be monitoring and reporting on progress and performance. In rare instances, it may only be possible to track annually (typically where the information source is external and only published once a year or is onerous to gather and annually is the only cost-effective approach). In many cases frequency will be monthly, the organisational default – long enough for the data to be meaningful but timely enough to spot trends and issues and act (at least in theory!). Challenge the conventional wisdom and consider where tracking trends or data weekly, even daily, would be more effective. Or if bi-monthly and quarterly is likely to yield more meaningful information. In all cases, consider the balance between producing meaningful insight, sometimes needing a longer measurement period, and remaining Agile enough to respond quickly.

Step 4 – For each improvement identified in Step 2, allocate the responsible person(s) in the firm. For the simplest approach, often most applicable in smaller firms (or practices/teams if running this exercise at that level), allocate a single 'owner' responsible for that objective. In more complex situations, consider using the RACI model developed for project management, identifying different individuals who need to be Responsible, Accountable, Consulted, Informed. This step is not just bland 'management consulting' box-ticking – it is a vital input to one of the later stages of the overall information/insight/impact model – intent. It is also a glaring gap in how many law firms define their management structures.

Step 5 – This step links impact to information. Based on the objectives identified and the measures suggested in Step 2 you should be able to list the sources of information you need to perform that measurement. Some of these will be obvious and conventional – and a lot of financial information will come directly from the firm's practice management system (PMS) or from reporting or BI suites that sit on top of your PMS. Other information may be stored in more niche sources, sometimes only used in one part of the firm. In the next section, information to intelligence, we outline examples of the common information sources in law firms in more detail. This may help you to complete Step 5, as it is not always obvious to management in the firm exactly where some important information sits – or whether it is available at all.

It is unusual, in my experience, for firms to approach issues of data and information with a blank sheet of paper – starting by identifying exactly what information they need. Too often, questions of data and information quality and coverage are entirely delegated to IT, information or finance teams who have great skills in managing databases and information systems but, in most cases, are less interested or educated in the next stages of how insights will be generated, decisions made and actions taken around the firm as a result. Firm leaders should personally engage with information and data as a critical asset of the firm and challenge the status quo that restricts what information you receive based on the arbitrary limitations of a specific PMS, whimsical personal preferences of your partners, or bold claims of legal technology salesmen.

When you review your own objectives and measures, following the five information steps above, seize that opportunity to check that they include all of the most fundamental goals and metrics that any business, whether a law firm or not, must include. I have spent a lot of my career working with professional firms on measuring and improving business performance and it continues to surprise me that the most basic business intelligence is sometimes missing. I have included here a cut-down extract from my 'business essentials' dimensions of performance (there is more of this, as well as the 'business next steps' checklist – the equivalent of a 'deeper cuts' playlist!). Business essentials are the fundamental questions that every business leader should always be able to answer in order to understand where the business is.

Table 1. Business essentials

What you sell.	Monthly, quarterly, annual turnover by practice area and product/service line (as well as 'sliced and diced' by team, office, sector etc). Always reflect profitability on same dashboard/report if possible – 'sales are vanity, profits sanity'.
What you generate.	Profit margin – gross margin after direct costs and realistic notional equity partner salary/remuneration (NEPS).
What you make.	Net margin – net margin after all costs (for client and large matter analysis this should ideally include cost of sales, include direct sales/marketing) and NEPS.
What clients value, like and dislike.	What aspects of your service do clients regard as most valuable and where is your service positively differentiated from competitors – constantly updated? What do you do – and not do – that clients dislike, find frustrating and introduce delay or distraction into their lives?
Which features of your service clients use most often.	Which tools, documents, communication and collaboration media, software and value-added services do clients use, and not use?
How busy people are.	Total time per individual/team/group average – include all time working (should match individual's total time contribution to firm, not 'chargeable only').
How productive people are.	Chargeable (plus any designated 'investment' categories that are value-add) time as percentage of standard working hours.
How much in the sales pipeline.	Sales pipeline analysis, highlighting target clients, work types and sectors. Tracked regularly.
What is capital 'lock-up'?	Identify healthy/necessary working capital levels and delayed/excess 'lock-up' and report aged 'lock-up' debt and work-in-progress.
How are we leaking revenue and profit?	For major matters at least track 'leakage' from total potential revenue and profit, split by time write-off, invoice discounting, bad debts, fixed fee/AFA over-run (latter is critical).
What is our client acquisition rate?	How many new clients are we creating (monthly/quarterly/annually), often quoted as a percentage of existing live clients?

What is our client churn rate?	How many clients do we lose (monthly/quarterly/annually), often quoted as a percentage of existing live clients? NB this is easiest to measure in retainer/subscription or recurring work practices. 'Returning clients within x years' may work better in less regular practices.
Where does new work come from?	Referrals and channels (external) identified for all major new opportunities. Do not allow tracking internal partner introductions to overshadow this activity. Should do both.
What rate are we charging?	Track *actual achieved rate* (after all write-offs, discounts etc) for matters and report against rate card.
What resource capacity do we have?	Rolling forward view (three months in detail, 12 months+ in outline) of lawyer resource based on current workload, matter plans, sales pipeline.
Are staff loyal and satisfied?	Attrition/turnover rates – percentage of staff leaving per annum; split between various 'good leaver'/'bad leaver' categories.

Stage 2: intelligence

Making data readable and usable – that is, converting it to information – is just the first step. What happens to that information to create intelligence? What most business applications now do in creating valuable outputs is a series of computational and intelligent processes that we used to rely on humans in finance and accounting, information services and other functions to do.
This conversion of information into intelligence includes the following activities:

- consolidation of data into period, group and category totals;
- comparison using stored prior period or budget comparatives;
- validation of data against pre-set rules and thresholds;
- calculation of variances, percentages and ratios;
- highlighting large or unusual results (often using colour);
- ordering results by size – using league tables or reporting only items over/under a specified amount;
- filtering results by a pre-set (or user-defined) criteria – to isolate the most relevant results for that user/practice/team etc;
- 'slicing and dicing' data based on different criteria to create an entirely new report tailored to a specific user's requirements;
- alerting users or system administrators in real-time or periodically to data that falls outside an agreed range or pattern (law firm PMS applications use these alerts a lot – for over-budget matters or due debts for example);
- triggering a workflow step or escalation by pushing an alert or report to a line manager or authoriser;
- visualisation of data into graphs, charts and infographics; and

- enriching base data with additional information from within the application – for example adding more standing data that provides context about the specified team/individual fee earner/client etc.

If you compile a directory of information sources in your firm at the information stage, you will probably find that these information-to-intelligence processes are happening mainly in a small number of core software applications on which you rely for most of your intelligence. The information to intelligence stage is mainly systems-driven. Particularly with the growing use of machine learning capabilities, most of the hard lifting that adds context, relevance and readability to raw data is performed as a core function by technology.

Within law firms the primary sources of intelligence are your practice management system (PMS) or enterprise resource planning (ERP) system; case or matter management systems; client relationship management (CRM) system; business intelligence (BI) tools; time recording systems; HR systems; payroll; document management system (DMS); email/Office platform; client and matter onboarding; Excel spreadsheets – especially those still being used by finance functions; niche and practice-specific applications; internal know-how databases; purchased knowledge platforms

"One of the big challenges law firms face in becoming insight-driven is a culture which can come very close to actively discouraging the revelation of new and different insights and perspectives on performance."

provided by the likes of Thomson Reuters, LexisNexis and Bloomberg; and external data sources including newsfeeds, search engines and social media.

The exact configuration of intelligence sources, the extent to which they are delivering contextual intelligence you can use and how well you are able to collate and connect these disparate sources will differ dramatically from firm-to-firm. While these are usually the primary sources, it is important to look beyond the obvious, firmwide systems to find some genuine nuggets of business insight.

Stage 3: insight
The stage at which intelligence is converted to insight can be described as 'where the magic happens'. For law firms it might be better described as 'where the magic *should* happen'. The creation of fresh and actionable insight from the reports, tables and charts that make up your firm's intelligence is not an area many management teams or partners have been focused on. Without that focus, law firms risk being uncompetitive in a competitive market, with some very data-savvy new entrants.

One of the big challenges law firms face in becoming insight-driven is a culture which can come very close to actively discouraging the revelation of new and different insights and perspectives on performance. Firms can become wedded to using particular strands of management information to determine often high-stakes profit distribution and this can produce, over time, a collective reluctance to explore different metrics that might give contradictory results. The most obvious example is that high levels of time recorded or fees billed – which can be the metric used to determine profit sharing – do not necessarily align with where most profit is generated for the firm. Every firm knows that time or fees are an imperfect proxy for profitability, but once the firm's remuneration, recognition and promotion processes become founded on fee generation, the organisation can become resistant to new ways of measuring profitability or allocating costs such as marketing, sales and write-downs. Professional firms can become myopic – rejecting the Agile principle of a continuous search for new insights into performance and indicators of weakness. Which is, of course, the essential ingredient to drive improvement and innovation.

Consequently, a critical component of the intelligence to insight phase comprises skilful communication, change management and partnership engagement. It is not easy to achieve a position where the entire firm becomes genuinely and enthusiastically 'insight-driven' – where every partner and manager in the firm is constantly pushing for deeper, better and more timely knowledge about team, practice, sector, firm and individual performance and acting on that insight. Also, where people demand insight before taking big management decisions about new clients, pricing, hires, resourcing and expect valuable intelligence 'on tap' – available in real-time and up to date.

Whereas the previous stage focused largely on deploying technology smartly to collate, combine and structure data for reporting purposes, this stage emphasises the importance of human labour working alongside digital labour. The advent of analyst, business intelligence, data scientist and pricing analyst roles in large law firms has been a big trend over the last few years. I expect that this is just the beginning of a new cohort of essential roles in the modern law firm. I have spoken to a number of legal recruiters over the last few years who see this skillset, alongside the legal engineer and process specialist, as their biggest growth area. Firm management teams need to understand better how to recruit and deploy these analysts and what the optimum blend of technology and people is.

Before you can begin to make those changes, you will want to be clear about what insight is. There are a few criteria that help distinguish insight from information or intelligence, mainly related to its value. Insight is:

- the result of systematic analysis – by human resources, technology or, commonly today, a combination of the two;
- extensive – typically multi-layered, pulling on multiple data sources and based on a series of 'what' questions, to get closer to the root cause;
- focused – insight is not generated by simply pushing out more reporting and information into the organisation. Analysts need to understand what the user/decision maker is trying to achieve and insight delivered should be focused tightly on that;
- predictive – simply reporting a historic metric does not create insight. Utilising that intelligence to suggest, anticipate or model a future outcome or trend does. An indication of what might happen next is more likely to trigger action from decision makers;
- usable and actionable – insights should be influential. Delivered in the right format, at the right time for the user and clearly explained, with the necessary supporting information for decisions to be made and action taken. That creates a crucial distinction compared to conventional information reporting.

Analysts and others involved in designing and then delivering insights to managers will often use established management tools, many of them closely connected with Agile methodologies, like

"The advent of analyst, business intelligence, data scientist and pricing analyst roles in large law firms has been a big trend over the last few years."

Root Cause Analysis and the Five Whys tool extensively used by Toyota – I will take a closer look at some of these tools later in the report. The purpose of using these methods at this point is to generate real insights that are not immediately obvious when you are presented with a static piece of information or intelligence; the insight is created by digging deeper, asking more questions, challenging the superficial or initial reading. That mining for nuggets of insight seldom happens in an environment which relies on standard-form financial reports being served up at the same time each month to the same over-busy individuals, without any premium being placed on finding new revelations and inconvenient facts.

Generating insight – the roles of technology and analysts
Generating great insights for your managers and decision makers does require good information as the raw material – firms that apply the i3 model often find that they don't get all the insights they need until they go back and fix the information sources that feed into intelligence and then insights.

The creation of insights that will drive business decisions and positive impact on your performance has to be the result of systematic analysis, rigorously focused on the required outcome and usable by decision makers and managers. Achieving that today without some substantial human analytical input is difficult, although the advent of more sophisticated business intelligence (BI) suites and integration of BI functionality into the bigger PMS and ERP applications means that legal software is gearing up to meet this challenge. This auto-analytics competence can deliver a substantial piece of the insight jigsaw-puzzle but still requires an investment of time and effort in scoping, design and maintenance – which means human skill and experience in analysis. Few law firms will find that their systems alone can generate genuine, actionable insights 'out-of-the-box'.

As at the end of 2019 there were over 350 individuals working in analyst, pricing officer and related roles in the big US and global law firms, as tracked by Patrick Johansen's influential 'Law Firm Pricing' website.[55] That is bound to be an underestimate, as pricing and profitability analytics has spread across the Atlantic to the big London firms and around the legal world. I think it is safe to declare that law firm analyst roles are poised to become mainstream.

What are these individuals doing? Information architects help in designing and leveraging the firm's information systems, ensuring that applications, databases, reporting and systems integration all work together to deliver the right information and intelligence that will generate insight. Most firms will have one or more people, typically in their IT function, with responsibility for data. Some large firms now have a chief data officer in place to lead this important area. However, these roles focus primarily on the underlying data architecture and on the rising priority issue of data security. It is the analysts who will have responsibility for the actual manipulation of information and delivery of insights.

Centralised analyst teams have been growing and prospering in larger law firms in recent years, as initial relatively modest investments in this skill-set have delivered a return. Some legal analysts bring data and statistical experience from outside the sector, others have grown up within legal and have legal and practice domain knowledge. As with other new Agile roles like legal project manager and legal engineer, many firms have concluded that a blend of people is ideal – some steeped in the legal industry and others who inject fresh ideas and different perspectives from other sectors. Traditionally, the finance function has often taken the lead in managing reporting and management information across the firm. I advise firms to encourage their finance team to develop and extend their delivery of insights, rather than just flat reporting for compliance and governance purposes, and to shift more resources to predictive analytics. However, the range of different metrics required by your firm encompasses much more than financial data (as shown by the business essentials table earlier in this chapter) and I do not endorse leaving firmwide responsibility for the i3 model/business intelligence in the hands of finance.

Many Agile organisations have developed an almost insatiable appetite for new intelligence and insight. This has fed into a trend for customer insights teams. I have seen some initial centralised law firm client insights teams and expect this to be a big development in the 2020s. These teams draw on all the potential sources of client understanding, including market research and the myriad big data outputs of web traffic and social media. This is a messier information role than the conventional financial and technology data and reporting jobs, with a strong emphasis on mining unstructured data and producing insights from an alchemical combination of multiple sources. But this is the job at the centre of mastering the information/insight/impact model in the new decade, requiring a new, more ambitious role for the client insight team which tries to make measurable sense of the constantly changing habits, attitudes and behaviours of your living, breathing, thinking, buying clients.

As the BI technology industry rapidly embraces artificial intelligence and machine learning capabilities and creates more Agile data

"I think it is safe to declare that law firm analyst roles are poised to become mainstream."

discovery tools, these powerful, cloud-based, mobile-enabled applications are democratising analytics. 'Citizen analysts' will soon be empowered to use natural language search and visual interfaces to mine very detailed and powerful insights. Law firms should be looking at how to develop the necessary interpretation, decision and change management skills across the organisation to make the most of this new asset. Hiring highly specialist central analytics resources should be augmented by efforts to develop localised, decentralised analytic competence in practices and teams.

Stage 4: intent
The i3 model is designed to ensure a flow through your firm from the data and information you spend substantial money, time and effort creating and storing through analysis that converts that into insight and, finally, to the pay-off – making decisions that create new client and business value. Without moving insights down the line to inform business decisions and then ensuring that those decisions are translated into effective, measurable action your return on the effort in the earlier stages of the model is going to be negligible.

The intent stage is where ability to make good decisions rapidly comes into play. It is the stage at which the firm takes insights and uses them to support business decisions – in an Agile firm that

"Day-to-day decision making needs to be informed by high-quality data, especially at the level of the Agile team."

should be a stream of small decisions taken regularly in response to the evidence, reflecting the principles of testing and iterating.

Take a new, critical look at the most important, valued and quoted information and metrics in your firm. Do these fully align with and support the Agile principles and client-centred focus? There should be a clear line of sight and no contradiction between the two. This is reinforced by what you choose to report, communicate and reward. Financial reporting often needs to be critically reviewed and redesigned to support your Agile aim. Day-to-day decision making needs to be informed by high-quality data, especially at the level of the Agile team (which firm reporting and management information mechanisms often under-serve). As I point out to most of the firms I work with, they spend a far higher proportion of their time and effort on analysis supporting decisions about allocating the profit they make than they do in supporting the decisions on how to deliver the service generating that profit.

Indeed, all the firm's internal systems and business support functions need to be aligned with and, more contentiously, subordinated to serving clients. If you find your firm's business support functions talking about and setting objectives exclusively for their internal customers you probably need to reconnect those people with your ultimate, external client. Back to that 'line of sight' phrase – the goals and activities of all the firm's component parts should be connected directly to the client.

There are eight key points I suggest firms consider and act on to get their decision making in shape:

- *Distribution* – identify which individuals and groups in the firm require which insights, how often, in which format – a critical element of designing any information process.
- *Decision rights* – often overlooked in the messy, status-centric world of the traditional partnership, this has nothing to do with 'who is a partner?'. Determining clearly who should have the responsibility and authority to make business decisions about pricing, hiring, business take-on, resourcing, expenditure, sales, client service changes etc is a critical feature of maximising the value and impact of intelligence and insight. The watchword is to get lots of the day-to-day decisions down to Agile teams who are close to the client.
- *Accountability* – ensure that there is clear 'line of sight' from the managing partner/CEO through the firm in terms of business performance ('impact') and that it is regularly measured. The Agile firm will have teams with a high level of autonomy but with that comes accountability and consequence.

- *Training* – part of any business training programme, ideally at all levels in the firm up to and including senior partner level, should be constantly updated skills in interpreting, understanding, flexing and acting on intelligence and insight. Law firm leadership and lawyer training programmes usually neglect these essential 21st-century competencies in my view.
- *Time to act* – the firm should reject the time-honoured rhythms of reporting that are usually derived from highly rigid 'rear-view mirror' financial accounting and profit distribution deadlines. These will not reflect the actual transaction and decision rhythms of your firm. Decision makers need information much more quickly and regularly than the usual reporting timetable. Similarly, major decisions based on insights should not wait until the next scheduled quarterly meeting or annual appraisal.
- *Bias to action* – professional firms are inherently inclined to non-intervention and to 'wait and see' approaches to change and difficult decisions. To combat this, firm leadership teams should push a 'bias to action' culture, that recognises and rewards 'doing something' in response to a new insight. This enshrines the Agile principle that promotes getting minimum viable product designs completed and out to clients to test and respond to and the underlying fundamental for Agile firms to respond quickly. Managing partners might introduce a requirement for practices, departments or teams to check-in periodically outlining the actions and changes they are making in response to each of their major KPIs, even where these are all being hit. This establishes the mindset that some response or change should always be in train, as opposed to the 'exception reporting' mindset where managers stay quiet – and change nothing – unless and until something is going wrong.
- *Document* – related to building a 'bias to action' firms should expect more documentation of variance analysis, decisions made and action required as part of day-to-day management. In Agile environments there is a strong emphasis on transparent, often highly visible and visual ways of showing activity and sharing that (think the Kanban boards discussed in the previous chapter). That doesn't require a great amount of formal reporting, especially with the advent of Agile, online systems which allow variances and intelligence to be annotated and shared in real-time.
- *Measures* – multiple perspectives and dimensions on a particular part of the firm, dimension of performance or market will provide the best insights. But simple and clean KPIs and dashboards are often the best tools to keep managers focused and able to see performance at-a-glance. This sets up a potential conflict – simple versus holistic – but I would always

exhort firms to explore as many different angles on their performance as possible, synthesising different sources of information into one measure where possible, while not feeling the need to enshrine all of these in your formal key performance indicator (KPI), objective or performance metrics.

Insight has to be converted quickly and seamlessly into intent via a smart, well-understood decision-making process. The way in which those insights are delivered up to decision makers can make or break this stage – and the entire i3 model. That delivery needs to ensure decision makers have the best chance of spotting insights and then quickly understanding and evaluating them. Using advances in application interfaces, the power of mobile and cloud technologies, personalisation of screens and layouts and flexible visualisation and presentation tools, there is now zero excuse for any firm to still be relying on printed or emailed 'flat' reports filled with row-upon-row of numbers. You will almost certainly need to tackle and overhaul your current reporting and information presentation to crack this stage. I have highlighted below a few ways in which insights can be served up more effectively.

Dashboards/portals – these are an attractive, simplified and regularly updated on-screen compendia of critical intelligence for a user, starting with their own KPIs. A smartly-designed dashboard ensures that all reporting is aligned with strategic goals and allows users to cut through the mass of financial and performance information and see, ideally 'at a glance', what is really important to them. Most modern BI and PMS applications output information gathered, sometimes from multiple sources, as dashboards. Careful design, training and communication plus regular updating can mean that the dashboard effectively converts intelligence into insight.

Client and market 'taxi pack' – a variant of the dashboard that assembles data around a specific client or market at pace from a variety of internal and external sources will often be one of the most popular insight outputs a firm can produce. Partners, business development and marketing professionals are hungry consumers of 'taxi-pack' briefing reports, predictive analytics on client buying and price behaviour and intelligence to support pitches and tenders.

Visualisation – an essential component of successful dashboards and insight-presentation, use of pictures, drill-down charts and infographics vastly enhances the usefulness and clarity of intelligence and insight provided. Catalysing insight into intent can be accelerated by using visual representation that taps into the neural networks and individual preferences of users more effectively.

Predictive analysis – this is especially valuable in matter management and analysis scenarios. Scoping and pricing matters can be done using tailor-made applications or generic software such as Microsoft Excel. Using historical matter data, budget estimates, matter plans and pricing options can be generated, with forecast profitability outcomes.

Alerts – most BI, PMS and reporting tools can deliver nuggets of insight in real-time on a 'just-in-time' basis, as well as through carefully constructed dashboards. This develops the well-established concept of building rules into line-of-business systems that will trigger alerts or notifications to users, eg when a financial or time-based threshold is reached, or a negative client feedback score is received. Extensive use of alerts, however, can lead to notification/email overload and ultimately impair not improve the organisation's ability to act quickly based on a timely insight. Smarter exception-based tools focus on only the most urgent and important triggers that require action and, in line with our prescription for insight, provide the layers of analysis and supporting information which make it easy for the user to act – rather than simply highlight that they need to investigate further themselves.

Agile BI – a self-service BI capability that users can utilise as and when they need insights, often delivering outputs to a range of devices, is increasingly essential. Releasing users from a reliance on hard-to-learn, desktop-bound enterprise systems or on passing all enquiries through a centralised and over-stretched BI team is often an important step in creating a workforce whose members become enthusiastic consumers and users of data-driven insights.

Stage 5: impact

Impact is best defined as delivering a demonstrable improvement in one or more of the key dimensions of your firm's business performance. This is the simple purpose of the extensive i3 process that collates very large amounts of data, uses expensive technology and human analytic skills to consolidate, filter and analyse it and then translates it into decisions and actions. Given that purpose the final stage of the information/insight/impact process is, clearly, critical.

Agile organisations have to be highly capable at taking actions that deliver the necessary change, improvement or movement that insights have suggested. This is about management of change – how well can the firm translate decisions quickly and efficiently into real impact.

For this stage there are eight key competencies your firm needs to have developed down to team and department level:

- *Measurement* – tracking the impact of decisions and actions.
- *Targeting* – estimation and calibration of the intended or likely extent of the impact from a single decision or action, or a group of them over a period.
- *Alignment* – maintaining a close relationship between the multitude of decisions and actions across the organisation and the strategic direction, plans and goals of the firm and individual unit.
- *Prioritisation* – determining how to allocate scarce resources (time, skill, money) to the multitude of needs and demands across the firm. Not attempting to do everything or leaving priorities to be set by who shouts loudest or 'games the system' best. This is critical to get right in an Agile environment, where you are simultaneously trying to extend the autonomy of teams to act and invest.
- *Portfolio and programme management* – effectively monitoring and supporting the overall portfolio of major actions, change programmes and investments being run by the firm at any one time.
- *Project management* – the ability to deliver a specific action or change to budget and timetable – specifically managing projects using Agile principles.

"Releasing users from a reliance on hard-to-learn, desktop-bound enterprise systems or on passing all enquiries through a centralised and over-stretched BI team is often an important step in creating a workforce whose members become enthusiastic consumers and users of data-driven insights."

- *Change management* – ensuring that changes are well communicated, explained, embedded and do not unnecessarily disrupt the organisation.
- *Operational effectiveness* – maintaining the business-as-usual running of all aspects of the firm, while successfully introducing changes and executing decisions (the 'changing the wheel while driving' skillset!).

The application of Agile principles in project management, innovation and change supports all of these points. This final step in the information/insight/impact model is often overlooked by the leaders in analytics and information technology who often feel their job is done if insights are delivered. Yet failure to effectively execute on those insights destroys their value and wipes out the ROI that firms expected when investing in the technology, data and analytic resources in the first place.

Agile first steps – insight-driven
- Implement the i3 model as a core management process at your firm, with a responsible senior process owner (ensuring you pay due attention to the intent and impact stages).
- Audit and identify your most valuable data assets, as well as the obvious gaps in your data and information sources (using the i3 model).
- Invest in creating valuable insights for your decision makers – use human analysts/BI specialists as well as enhanced BI tools.
- Redesign decision rights and decentralise and devolve the responsibility for making more of your business decisions – ensuring these people have the tools and insights they need.
- Ensure that your firm can answer the business essentials questions in full.

V. Highly autonomous teams

1. Agile and the liquid workforce

Agile organisations are all based on a foundation of the network of empowered teams. Those teams are ideally small, multi-disciplinary and self-managing. Law firms sometimes feel more confident at the prospect of adopting Agile practices when they first hear this because law firms are pretty good at setting up small teams focused on a specific area of work or type of client. That structure has evolved primarily from a tradition that is more individualistic than team-based – the partnership. Individual partners are expected and backed to grow their own team. In classic law firm theory, they will leverage a pyramid of junior lawyers and build their profit-generating capacity and earnings potential. This is *not* the same team ethos and dynamic that a new business aiming to run Agile is creating, but the fact remains that law firms are often, intrinsically, networks of small teams.

In some firms that networked team structure is obscuring what often remains essentially an individual pursuit. The org chart may show neat rows of teams but the reality on the ground is a mix of individuals working mainly solo, small cliques and the occasional fully-functioning team, often in practice areas where fixed fees and tight margins have forced the team together into a better-functioning and more efficient unit. Adopting Agile methods will provide an opportunity to challenge and tackle this pervading individualism if it affects your firm and get it working in a much more collaborative and efficient way.

Although we operate structures that already break down naturally into teams, law firm teams – especially in the larger corporate firms – can be too big to operate in the self-managing Agile model, working intently on client-focused sprints. Teams may need to be broken down further into smaller units to support the Agile methods outlined in this and the previous few chapters. These smaller Agile units can be continuously flexed, coming together for specific matters and projects, subdividing and then reforming as required, based on the size and shape of matters the team is working on. In the law firm environment, it is seldom practical for these smaller Agile units to be formed and remain fixed for very long periods, unless there is a very regular, steady intake of matters of similar size and scope.

The key point here is to loosen up the idea that your practice group structures have to be fixed, formal and permanent. Some big benefits can flow from implementing an Agile, responsive approach to team formation and reformation. Your people get a wider range of experience of different types of matter, working with a regularly changing cast of colleagues, sometimes alongside specialist professionals they would not get so close to in the conventional silo and function-based structure.

"Law firm teams – especially in the larger corporate firms – can be too big to operate in the self-managing Agile model, working intently on client-focused sprints."

The firm's physical space needs to flex in order to support the regular coming together and dissolution of Agile teams. This is something the big accounting and consulting firms recognised years ago and which we have seen 21st-century law firm office design increasingly provide – project spaces and rooms, touchdown desks, fluid desk composition. Although the usage stats for these facilities in law firm offices has often disappointed. Many firms believe the ability to co-locate Agile teams flexibly facilitates the Agile journey and boosts productivity. Often, however, and certainly in the wake of the 2020 pandemic, this physical co-location is not going to be feasible. Firms have begun to find effective digital ways of simulating the Agile team 'space', now putting their effort into enabling effective remote working, by-passing the physical obstacles to working in Agile teams that traditional cellular offices represent.

One other key feature of the Agile team is its multi-disciplinary make-up. This puts a premium on diversity of thought, experience and ideas in solving increasingly complex challenges in a VUCA world. Some law firms have gone a little way down this line by embedding technology, HR, finance, document production, innovation and other specialists at practice level, but few have assigned those resources to teams. Not every skill will be needed for every matter or project, but the key is that they are available and can be integrated into the multi-functional team, rather than sit outside of it. The principle here is to embed the skills and know-how in the teams that work directly with clients, where it is needed, as close to the client as possible, rather than having to stop everything and wait for an issue to be reviewed and resolved by another function or someone in a central team who is not working to the faster rhythm of Agile.

Law firms will need to come to terms with this idea of the modern liquid workforce – an Agile workforce with a kinetic mix of expert skills formed into teams to work around projects. Resourcing is refocused on developing blended teams which have a much more fluid combination of employees, freelancers/contractors, specialist consultants and outsourced service providers. The liquid model is going to replace the siloed, functional environments we have been accustomed to. One consequence of this is that resource planning competence and the technology applications that support it are becoming a critical part of the law firm armoury.

2. Designing the Agile network of teams
In *The Age of Agile*, Steven Denning notes that to create an ecosystem of autonomous teams you need to rethink your key organisational principles: "if you want individuals to think and behave like owners, the organization must be decomposed into small, localized units – each with its own profit and loss (P&L) responsibility".[56] Yes, one of the

leading gurus and evangelists of the Agile organisation is telling corporates to reconstruct themselves to look more like an archetypal law firm. It reminds me of one of the key lines I used back in the early 2000s when presenting to audiences on law firm management:

> *we need to resolve the contradictions of a new generation of law firm leaders and business professionals trying to get their firms to behave more like traditional corporations, just as the most enlightened corporations are trying to work out how to behave more like partnerships.*

That ironic statement is central to the question of how to create an Agile law firm. It contains a warning to protect against the corrosive impact of apparently sensible, but possibly already outdated, business processes practices borrowed from other industries.

In Agile organisations, governance becomes far more hands-on and real-time, with more decisions being made at the client interface. This will take day-to-day decisions away from central senior leadership. Rather than ask senior leadership to actively manage how well teams collaborate with each other, as well as with partners beyond the boundary of the organisation, Agile firms should look to build a culture which operates like a perpetual motor of collaboration, with incentives, reporting and strategy all aligned to stimulate it.

Teams generally work without interruption. The phrase 'self-managed' is important. The expectation of each Agile team is to direct itself – setting goals and completing sprints. This environment is built on trust, mutual reliance and a no-blame ethos. It is not always easy to achieve and making the journey towards becoming an Agile firm can expose the skin-deep nature of trust in any firm. You may have experienced something of the same painful but, ultimately, cathartic and positive debate over trust during 2020 as staff at all levels and in all job types were suddenly working alone from home, without any of the traditional forms of visual supervision we are used to. Denning makes it clear that this is a big shift in mindset and behaviour: "control is enhanced by letting go of control, and Agile leaders are less like fierce, conquering warriors than curators or gardeners".[57]

The autonomous team model challenges the persistent orthodoxy that a top-down model and hierarchical structure is necessary to achieve big things. Organisations have always tended to reach a certain scale and assume that more authority and autonomy needs to be sucked away from teams in order to plan and achieve more ambitious goals. However, instead of constructing a big and complex organisation to handle complex issues, the Agile organisation disaggregates them into much smaller parts that can be handled by small teams in short cycles.

"The Agile model suggests that a network of small teams can solve bigger, more complex problems just as well as having a structure of larger, fixed teams."

Can the small team principle really scale? The Agile model suggests that a network of small teams can solve bigger, more complex problems just as well as having a structure of larger, fixed teams. The key is truly effective collaboration – building a fluid and dynamic ecosystem.

3. Evolving teams into Agile teams

Simply organising as small teams is not the answer to becoming Agile, of course. Developing truly Agile teams requires much more than a tweak of the structure chart or a bit of relabelling. Most of the Agile champion organisations referred to at the beginning of this report have taken years to build their Agile culture. In this short section I will outline some of the most important characteristics of Agile teams.

The application of truly Agile working is based around the sprint. A project is broken down into a series of sprints – each one focused on a critical objective. This contrasts with the traditional Waterfall development methodology, in which all activities are tackled sequentially and in which a delay at one stage can create a backlog and wasted resource down the line.

The target of a sprint, the sprint goal, is decided on between the product owner and the team. The sprint is a concentrated effort to produce an output that can be put into practice immediately.

The team plans sprints in advance, deciding what work can get done in this sprint and how the chosen work will get done.

As the word would imply, an Agile sprint is like a short race. They typically take place in a period of no more than two to four weeks. At Microsoft, the standard rhythm of three-week sprints continues even through holidays. Although it is a lighter sprint in terms of work content, the timing doesn't change – the teams like the consistent rhythm. However, sprints in the legal context and in other industries, could be shorter or longer, depending on the type of work and size of team. In legal teams the sprint will often be structured around milestones or defined phases of a matter.

In Agile and the Scrum approach that puts its principles into action sprints provide focus and help teams increase the pace of delivery – addressing velocity, one of the main Agile objectives. The team is focused intently on one sprint and one outcome (sprint goal) at one time. Getting that done, promptly and efficiently, is everything. Large, bureaucratic organisations tend to have piles of part-done tasks and activities, habitually taking on too many at once.

Daily stand-ups (also referred to as 'daily scrums') bring the whole team together, briefly, to assess what work has been done, what will be done next, what issues have been encountered and how to deal with them. The goal of this meeting is to surface any blockers that impact the team's ability to deliver the sprint objective.

Best practice is to run these meetings at the same time each day (most run in the morning) for 10–15 minutes. Discipline is critical – these are not general 'catch-up' team meetings.

Backlog is another key feature of the Agile model. The term might suggest something that has gone wrong, but it is simply the label for the sum total of all the work that the team needs to complete at any point in time. That work is comprised of what Agile refers to as *user or client stories* (which you might also refer to as 'client requirements or needs' or 'client outcomes'). Instead of writing a specification for a new feature that describes it in technical terms, the Agile approach requires a story that describes the feature from the point of view of the client, using plain language.

It is essential that the backlog is constantly maintained, curated and prioritised – this is not a 'nice to have' as it might be in parts of your firm today! The Agile team should have full visibility of the backlog and it is the focus of planning. Those client stories will usually be broken down into trackable tasks that will take one identified person, or sometimes two working together, up to a day to perform.

"The Agile team should have full visibility of the backlog and it is the focus of planning."

Burndown chart is a graph that shows how much work is left to be done and how much time is left to do it. This allows you to estimate and visually communicate when the work in the backlog will be done. The chart can act as an early red flag if things are backing-up or you're falling behind schedule.

Work in progress limits is an Agile term that might be confusing in the law firm environment, which already uses 'WIP' to refer to unbilled work done for clients. In the Agile context the term simply refers to the amount of work (measured in tasks) still to be done by the team. Over time, the team learns how much work they can expect to handle at any one time and a WIP limit can be defined which identifies the maximum. In conjunction with the backlog and burndown chart, WIP limits are used to regulate the tap of new work and drive constant reprioritisation.

Metrics – Agile demands constant, 'radical' transparency. Information on the status of work is universally available – typically up on the walls, but now perhaps more likely to be onscreen, in screen-saver dashboards and dashboards. This is not rear-view mirror financial data on fees, chargeable hours or origination, this is real-time data on how the team is doing in achieving its client work.

Coaching – many leading companies have deployed Agile coaches throughout their business to educate, nurture, support and trouble-shoot. Coaches, though they support a specific group of teams, are not managers. There is typically some deliberate distancing of the coach from the team – with the coach having a number of teams to support and not being co-located. The team can be weaned off the need for regular coaching support over time and become fully self-managing and independent. That is not simple to achieve, as many Agile organisations will attest, especially when teams hit hard times and performance dips – when the coach is most likely to be pulled back in.

Management – Agile team managers are not bosses. But, of course, in many circumstances people who have previously been managers remain in place in the Agile organisation, continuing to contribute their higher-level skills and expertise to the multi-disciplinary effort. That adjustment for former managers, and senior employees of all kinds, is never going to be easy or straightforward. Some organisations have recognised the need to place much greater emphasis on training and educating managers in the new Agile working practices.

The fundamental mindset managers need to adopt here is often described as *servant leadership* – a shift away from command and control. They provide expert advice, support and help the team deal

"Law firms, however, are mostly built on a legacy of traditional partnership structures with a partner building, growing and unambiguously leading their own team."

with obstacles. This is by no means alien to law firms, of course. Many partners and directors in legal firms are personally inclined to act as highly supportive, nurturing 'servant leaders' for their team. Law firms, however, are mostly built on a legacy of traditional partnership structures with a partner building, growing and unambiguously leading their own team. Teams are often simply referred to by the name of their partner and 'my team' with the emphasis on 'my' rather than 'team' is the way some partners still refer to their co-workers. This model has worked well for many people (though by no means all – too often the partners simply are not good leaders or managers or talented young lawyers are constrained under a too-restrictive regime) for many years. But it is not Agile and it is under increased pressure from multiple forces in the 21st century, not least the very different attitudes and expectations of Gen Z.

Among the challenges of establishing Agile teams in the law firm environment, a big obstacle is a hierarchical culture. Given how critical to Agile team working the rituals like sprints, daily stand-ups, post-matter debriefs are, it is never going to be acceptable for one or two people in the team to decide to opt out, or to dominate the proceedings. Some legal partnerships are not inherently hierarchical and some partners naturally play a whole-hearted team player role. But that is not the case with all partners or in all firms and any firm 'going Agile' has to be prepared to work hard to combat the potentially very negative impact of retaining all the trappings of conventional hierarchy.

Senior management and central functions cannot afford to opt-out either. It is all too common for Agile principles and transformation to be rolled-out at the team level with little change happening at the top of the organisation. At the very least, senior management should be adopting some of the key principles of Agile working – 'walking the talk'. These changes could include:

- refocusing management agendas, plans and priorities around client value outcomes and away from primarily internal objectives;
- senior managers adopting coaching responsibilities and eliminating purely 'command and control' relationships as they do so;
- using Agile project management methodologies, including tools like Kanban boards, to visualise and plan their own work; and
- replacing traditional senior management meetings with daily stand-up huddles, focused on the Agile projects.

Purpose – one of the important, but easily overlooked, foundations of Agile teams is that every team member feels they are engaged in

"One of the important, but easily overlooked, foundations of Agile teams is that every team member feels they are engaged in work that really matters and is meaningful to them personally."

work that really matters and is meaningful to them personally. Law firms have an easy head-start on many other types of business here. A large amount of legal work has a significant impact on the lives of clients and other connected parties. Some of it has wider societal, financial or political significance too, beyond the individual case or client. Many other industries simply do not have that intrinsic wider purpose and do not attract people, as law does, with a strong sense of vocation. What is less clear to me, is whether everyone involved in delivering that legal work generally feels that the work is meaningful for them and that their contribution to the team effort is defined and appreciated. One of the aims of Agile teams is to allocate work and define individual contributions in a way that this personal sense of purpose is stimulated.

Accountability – in the software industry, one of the revelations of embracing Agile was the reallocation of responsibility for handling bugs and errors back to the development team. Many companies had built a separate team to bug-fix and get software ready to ship, but these teams were hardly invested in or inspired by their work; they had no involvement in building the code they were fixing. And the originating developers were often not measured or incentivised on the usable quality of their output – there are parallels here in firms who measure their fee-earning lawyers based on hours of input and don't reflect whether work has to be written off or clients complain further down the line. By putting bug-fixing back into the team's remit this has changed. Some companies, following the Toyota production system, will simply halt all work on anything new or the next sprint in order to sort out bugs.

This is the ultimate expression of genuinely self-managed teams and has obvious potential parallels for lawyer teams. Until any complaints are dealt with and resolved, bills issued, final client check-in done, matter closed and stored securely and in full, work on the next file should not take precedence. These things are not 'somebody else's job' – a client-centric firm will recognise that they often mean a lot more and loom much larger for the client, whereas lawyers can sometimes dismiss them as 'admin'.

Agile first steps – highly autonomous teams
- Review your org chart, identifying where your structure is too rigid or teams too large to support a self-managing small teams model.
- Find at least three ways to stimulate more Agile team behaviours in legal and support areas – focus on increasing teamwork and communication, reducing reliance on hierarchy.
- Replace as many individual targets and measures as you can with team alternatives.
- Lead from the front by running your team and others that are prominent in the firm as Agile teams, using the 'evolving teams into Agile teams' section.
- Identify a group of partners/senior managers from across the firm who are ready to adopt Agile team working and the servant leadership model ahead of the rest of the firm.

VI. The human dimension

1. Valuing individuals

In the Agile firm we want individuals to think and behave like owners. At its best Agile is a very different way of thinking about – and then putting into practice – how human beings collaborate with each other to achieve great things. Agile organisations tap into not only the unquenchable human motivation to do things that will impress and delight others, but also the power of pulling together people who enjoy doing this and have a similar mindset to work together in high-achieving teams.

The human dimension in Agile is right there in the original Agile Manifesto (Agile Alliance, 2001). Article One reads: "[we value] individuals and interactions over processes and tools".[58] Throughout the Agile principles there is a continued emphasis on the personal and individual – watchwords include collaboration, face-to-face communication, motivation and purpose. This is, let's not forget, a statement originally drafted to announce a new way of developing software – it is a long way from the tech-centric process that many imagine Agile to be. People, not technology, not process, are at the heart of Agile. That is something not well understood. Fear of using process, analytics, technology and techniques honed in industrial and digital sectors continues to make many lawyers reluctant to take a closer look. That Agile is all about people may be the single most important takeaway for any reader of this report.

I have referenced the human attribute of Agile a number of times already in this report. It surfaced strongly in discussing the tools and techniques used to support innovation and improvement, especially design thinking, often described as 'human-centred design'. Words that express intrinsically human values are to the fore in the Agile methodology. The language of Agile, emphasising empathy, authenticity, transparency, curiosity and continuous learning is significantly more people-centred, human and engaging than the language law firms employ. The emphasis on revenue-generation and utility at the source of terms law firms use most often when talking about their people has made me wonder for over 20 years if it reveals the true, underlying culture and priorities of firms. I have alternatives for all of these terms that I use whenever I can but in most firms you simply cannot avoid references to 'fee earners', 'chargeable time', 'fee targets', 'profit per equity partner', 'utilisation' and 'realisation'. If Agile versus traditional law firm was a contest to demonstrate a genuine belief in the individual and duty of care for your people and your clients, as expressed through the language and measures you use, Agile wins every time.

Law firms do pride themselves on being 'people businesses' and most leaders I have worked with do, genuinely, put a lot of emphasis on their people. This view is borne out by some external benchmarks. In the United Kingdom, law firms are regularly placed in the top companies to work for and best place to work lists, with law over-represented as a sector. These accolades, and similar plaudits for lawyers in other countries and regions, are won despite an acknowledged hard-working, high-stress and long-hours culture – something that is getting more attention in an era when mental health has received a lot more attention.

Not everybody finds working for a law firm easy or enjoyable, of course. One thing I hear often from HR directors and C-suite executives in law firms is that there is a growing challenge to meet the expectations of different generations and demographics inside today's firms. There is a sense that big law firms have taken too long to wake up and act on diversity and inclusion. While women in the profession have, in recent years, become an overall majority in many jurisdictions, the percentage of female partners and leaders remains comparatively low. Some progress in attracting more lawyers from a wider range of ethnicities and social backgrounds is, similarly, not reflected at the most senior levels. Firms are still accused of being hierarchical, elitist and cliquey and there are some pockets of the profession where that description would still be seen as a badge of pride!

To achieve the speed of movement, intense focus on client outcomes and the autonomous, self-managed team model of Agile, the traditional law firm culture will need to change even faster. Some quite fundamental components of the traditional model need to be deconstructed before Agile can truly flourish.

2. Becoming more human in the 2020s
During the COVID-19 pandemic, we all had to grapple with different ways of working with team-mates, other colleagues and clients. The emphasis on natural, highly collaborative human contact that runs through this report was put under severe strain.

Technologies we had begun to use, but only tentatively and irregularly before COVID-19 struck, have now become second nature, even if our use of them is rudimentary. We have drafted in Zoom, Teams, Slack, eSignatures to a prominent place in daily working lives very suddenly, without much time for reflection on best practices, training or avoiding negative side-effects. For many, how we use these tools has barely evolved since we first turned them on in the spring of 2020. As a result, much of their potential to actually enhance, rather than dilute human interaction is unexplored. The legal world needs a collective effort to identify, disseminate and leverage the positive 'humanising' potential of these tools.

Ways of working changed dramatically in 2020, as we all know. Not all the outcomes of the sudden switch to working from home were positive. Anyone working from a cramped or crowded apartment, back-bedroom or kitchen table; juggling child or elder care with work calls; or even just facing a daily struggle against poor broadband will attest to the negative impacts that a sudden, and then extended, expulsion from the office can have. Many have found working hours extended and the important, protective barrier between home and work time under assault or lost entirely. There are lots of issues to resolve if, as seems certain, the legal world adopts a much more hybrid and Agile way of working permanently going forward.

While the isolation of working remotely has made work less enjoyable, sociable and comfortable for many people, there have been big strides in building the foundations of more human, Agile organisations. One area of progress has been in adapting working patterns and schedules more sensitively to different personal and domestic circumstances. Colleagues have found ways of scheduling key calls and activities that fit around the various domestic activities each has to fit into their day, often engaging in a new level of collaboration and joint planning to make this work. Without the need to allow for commuting and travel time, days can be rescheduled to ensure that both work and key domestic duties – making breakfast, school run, kid's bath-time – can be accommodated.

"Despite the best efforts of many people inside and outside law firms, that office-first, long hours culture ingrained with suspicion of flexibility in time, place or role, has been tough to change."

The '9 to 5', presenteeism culture that still pervaded law firms, even those which considered themselves flexible and Agile, has taken a mortal hit. That blow has been a long time coming and offers the potential to sweep away some of the most stubborn, constricting and damaging aspects of how lawyers work. Despite the best efforts of many people inside and outside law firms, that office-first, long hours culture ingrained with suspicion of flexibility in time, place or role, has been tough to change. A failure to genuinely diversify the profession, particularly to open up the most senior echelons to enough women and individuals from different social and ethnic backgrounds, has allowed these cultural norms to prosper (maybe that should read 'fester') for longer in the shadows of the legal industry than they have in some other sectors.

2020 saw a dramatic surge in daily, habitual use of communication apps with video as the default choice for connecting with clients and colleagues. It has been called the 'Zoom Boom', though not only Zoom but also Microsoft Teams have emerged as huge winners. Both added daily users in the 10s and then 100s of millions during 2020. Working habits have veered suddenly and dramatically from face-to-face meetings, punctuated by audio-only phone calls, to remote meetings using video. There are restrictions to the full adoption of video meetings, poor bandwidth, privacy and safeguarding concerns (especially in education settings), and limitations to take-up in older or underprivileged demographics. However, video has become a default channel for most internal and many external communications in the legal sector. Zoom is the new meeting room and that demands firms give full consideration to the facilities, environment, protocols and etiquette that apply to these new spaces from where we run the majority of our meetings. Taking just one example – norms for working attire will need to be discussed and clarified as we move further into our post-pandemic lives; are employees going to be trusted to present themselves appropriately – and assess whatever that means in the 2020s – or are guidelines, coaching, even policing all required?

For all the concerns having video meetings enter our homes might have engendered, there are some positive implications for our human interaction. Calling using video as the default, rather than audio only, creates a greater degree of interaction with individuals and enables multi-user team calls that have at least some of the feel and form of in-person meetings. Body language is such a fundamental component of how we communicate with each other and the move towards video intrinsically builds that into our remote engagement with colleagues and contacts.

Beyond the basic functions of connecting people remotely using video and/or audio, these popular communication apps have a hinterland of features that are, as noted, barely being used in most firms. The 'chat' channels capability in Teams, akin to the popular features of tools such as Slack and Google Hangouts, has begun to be harnessed by some law firms to facilitate matter-related collaboration and communication. International law firm Osborne Clarke now automatically creates a Teams channel for each new matter opened. Integration into other features of the Microsoft stack, especially calendar and email, or with other third-party apps is going to be a key battleground for Teams and Zoom in the early 2020s. Training and coaching of users that expands their day-to-day connectivity and productivity are going to be equally important, taking the adoption of these connecting tools beyond the reflex usage patterns established in the immediate pandemic response.

Mental health, already mentioned above, is in the spotlight at long last and I expect it to remain so for the rest of the decade. I hope we will make rapid progress on really concrete ways in which this problem can be tackled in our corner of the business world. There is little doubt that on the preventative side law firms have a lot to do to ensure that their working patterns, management style and method of measuring performance are not directly contributing to mental ill health. Being able to accommodate a much wider range of working styles and schedules and recognising and adapting to different lifestyles will be very important. But firms can also turn the positive, 'best place to work' aspect of their cultures to good use as well. As organisations that often put a focus on the individual, firms can emphasise their agility by supporting a wide range of different ways of working, celebrating diversity within the context of strong teams and communities. Leaders need to show leadership in this area – recognising the challenges they personally have and the need to get themselves in order first before leading others.

3. Rethinking our relationship with employees – adopting the EACH model

Lucy Adams is a UK-based consultant and former senior HR executive who writes and speaks extensively on how HR needs to change in the modern world. She draws on her learning from a number of senior roles, including at the BBC and, before that, at international law firm Eversheds. In her book *HR Disrupted*[59] she lays out a framework for revolutionary change in the way organisations deal with their people. It is a framework I have returned to many times in my legal consulting work and it is an excellent exploration of what the people dimension of an Agile transformation should look like.

Lucy's work responds to the multiple challenges that organisations are facing, many of which have also contributed to the development of Agile itself. These include flexible working patterns, the gig economy, multi-generational workforces, the decline of trust, rise of collaboration, dealing with ambiguity and, prophetically, managing virtual teams.

The EACH model is at the core of *HR Disrupted*.[60] It is a simple 'formula' that advocates treating Employees (E) as Adults, Customers and Human beings (ACH). At first glance it sounds pretty obvious – why wouldn't we treat our employees as adults and humans? Law firms, proud of being 'people businesses' may well feel that they already tick these boxes. But a closer look generates some big questions about just how *human* your firm is.

3.1 Employees as adults

So much about management behaviour, not least in law firms, unconsciously reverts to the parent-child model. Think for a minute about the policy announcements your firm produces in areas such as compliance, finance, HR and IT. These tend to be written and then communicated and followed up (maybe you say 'policed') as if either the employee needs protecting, like a child, or the firm needs protecting from the employees (often including partners) who are likely to go rogue and misbehave. These are intrinsically parent-child behaviours transcribed to the work environment. Of course, individuals do make mistakes or fail to follow rules and that can generate risk. But we have a habit of legislating for the 1% who regularly do this and treating the 99% of the grown-ups who make up our firm like children. The habit is self-fulfilling – over time we have created an expectation of a certain style of decision making, communication, policing and monitoring from the centre. This cycle has to be broken in order to build the self-managed, highly autonomous teams that sit at the heart of Agile working.

To make a clear shift towards treating employees as adults, firms need to re-examine every step in this process from deciding whether a policy or communication is even required to how it is monitored and infractions are dealt with. Training programmes need to be reconsidered, putting emphasis on supporting personal and team self-management. And trust needs to be placed, very prominently, at the centre of the relationship. Many firms have had to reappraise trust in their working relationships in the wake of the massive surge in remote, home working since 2020. The aim now should be to secure those 'gains' and move onto a 'next level' of mutual, adult-to-adult relationships.

There is another angle to Agile organisations treating their people as adults. It revolves around using many of the Agile toolkit of techniques

"Many firms have had to reappraise trust in their working relationships in the wake of the massive surge in remote, home working since 2020."

and approaches I feature throughout the report. Most of the Agile methodologies focus on making the client experience more streamlined and effortless. But the same techniques can and should deliver a transformed employee experience too. Deploying lessons from Lean, Six Sigma and design thinking the processes and workflows your people use can be dramatically overhauled. This is not just a nice to have by-product of improving the client journey, it is a valuable end in itself. Staff quickly get tired of hearing leaders of apparently Agile organisations endlessly repeat the mantra of client centricity but not deal with the illogical and inefficient processes, practices and systems they have to use internally. People want to know 'what's in it for me'? There is no reason why the Agile journey should not yield streamlined, simplified and less effortful working lives for all of your people. If we stopped wasting our people's time, what could they do with it?

3.2 Employees as customers

From the perspective of an Agile transition, a commitment to consciously treating all of your people as customers/clients is little short of genius. The founding principles at the heart of the Agile firm that place empathy, client-centricity and an obsession with delivering value to clients will be embedded much more deeply if the same approach is applied to all of your people. There are three objectives – and associated actions – around treating your people as customers.

- By applying the same attention, 'getting to know you' and relationship-building effort you use to get to know your clients (see the client-centricity section above) to your people, the firm can establish a new, more tailored and personalised engagement with employees.
- Central teams and senior management should adopt Agile working to the same extent as client-facing teams, by taking the customer-centric approach to internal changes and innovation and engaging 'internal customers' directly in the design and iteration process your firm's Agile journey will be accelerated and deepened.
- Your client-facing teams should be experiencing what your clients will, informing the innovation and improvement they then apply to client service, having experienced 'life through the client's eyes'.

3.3 Employees as human beings

This final part of the 'human' trilogy is the one that tends to generate the most initially dismissive reactions. Of course, your firm treats its people like human beings! Just look at all of those awards and commendations I mentioned earlier in the section.

Beneath the surface, though, I think there is a reflex to dehumanise

"Staff quickly get tired of hearing leaders of apparently Agile organisations endlessly repeat the mantra of client centricity but not deal with the illogical and inefficient processes, practices and systems they have to use internally."

many of the key touchpoints between the firm and its people. There is too much depersonalised language, bureaucracy and administration in key 'human' touchpoints such as performance and pay reviews, an overuse of financial information as a proxy for real analysis of performance and minimal attention paid to the authentic 'voice' of the client.

Lucy Adams is critical of businesses for failing to pay serious attention and apply even the simplest of lessons from the mass of recent, highly persuasive psychological and neuroscience insight into how the human brain works and responds to communication, engagement, stress and other stimuli. She has a great point here and any successful firmwide pivot to an Agile state is going to require careful consideration and smart application of this kind of research. Some of the first steps in this direction are disarmingly simple: at one point in her book, Lucy advises managers, "next time you create a PowerPoint presentation, have a go at stripping out most of the numbers".[61] As she comments, it might make you feel uncomfortable but that is going to be true of most of the efforts you will need to make to make a break from the historic relationship with employees.

4. The servant leader

People are at the centre of every Agile organisation and successful organisational agility means all the people in the firm are engaged and empowered, not just a few. This is not simply about ensuring that partners, or all lawyers, or all people above a certain rank, have some additional autonomy. The whole organisation needs to be empowered. The mindset, skillset and guiding principles of entrepreneurs are what Agile organisations look to instil right across their firms.

Servant leadership is a strong principle supporting Agile working. Leaders are coaches, visionaries and communicators more than they are controllers, directors, planners.

Agile firms have to be high trust environments, not reliant on scores of policies, rules and supervision. Rather than information is power, collaboration is founded on the principle that sharing information is power. An organisation that is siloed and hierarchical in its reporting structure and communications style is not one in which trust is easily created. Not do these organisations usually feel compelled to respond quickly to change. Silos create barriers that separate 'us' from 'them' so that communications take longer and collaboration often has to be requested or incentivised.

"People are at the centre of every Agile organisation and successful organisational agility means all the people in the firm are engaged and empowered, not just a few."

5. Agile performance management
An Agile firm will also need to review and reinvent the processes and practices that impact on people most directly – especially around performance. Many organisations have abandoned restrictive annual budgeting and performance management approaches, for example, and adopted rolling, regular and dynamic Agile planning, budgeting and review. I will take a brief look in this section at how these tools can be applied in law firms.

The 'no appraisal' movement has gained ground in the last five years or so. It is by no means restricted to organisations that would describe themselves as Agile, but there is synergy between the roll-call of companies who have scrapped the annual appraisal and Agile champions. Without a doubt the move towards a more fluid, just-in-time and responsive system of engaging with employees is symptomatic of more organisational agility.

Dell, Microsoft, IBM, Gap, Accenture and General Electric have all ditched the annual appraisal. A lot of consulting and business thinkers' time has gone into evaluating the net benefit or impact of performance reviews, but few studies suggest that there is a decent return on the substantial amount of time and effort that goes into the process. In law firms that investment falls heavily on very busy fee-earning partners and the circus of diary management, documentation (especially where performance touches on partner remuneration or associate promotion) and chasing-up is often onerous and exhausting.

The Agile approach to managing performance resets the traditional annual appraisal and is gaining ground in the legal industry. The following key features give a good idea of the Agile model and how it differs from the conventional process.

- Language is recalibrated – appraisal, performance review, ratings are all removed in favour of terms that emphasise the mutual, constructive and action-orientated nature of the activity (eg, simply 'review', 'conversation', 'evaluation', 'planning session'); performance development not performance management.
- Discussions are regular and timely – ideally, they happen shortly after a key event (which could be negative or positive, or simply be the end of a large matter or project) but should happen throughout the year.
- The discussion is verbal and in-person, though this will probably increasingly be done by video.
- The discussion and evaluation is two-way, with a focus on the appraisee leading the review with their self-assessment.
- Ratings and gradings are not used, as they easily subvert the

aim of an open and two-way conversation about performance and lead to everything apart from the pronouncement of the rating (typically at the end) not being heard, or actioned.
- The discussion is informed by a spectrum of data and insights, not restricted to financial data, available and reviewed by all parties ahead of the meeting.
- For every client-facing employee and partner the first and most important area for review and source of evidence is client service delivery and client satisfaction. Even for business support staff, their direct and indirect interaction with clients should be an area of focus.
- Objectives should be few in number, focused and SMART (specific, measurable, achievable, relevant, timed). They should be reviewed more than annually and always be fully aligned with team plans and objectives, Agile sprints and other interconnected goals.
- The appraiser(s) should adopt a coaching approach as much as possible, assisting with self-evaluation, highlighting key insights from the evidence (as opposed to 'well *I think* that....') and ensuring the discussion constantly returns to action, improvement and development.
- Bottom drawer syndrome – objectives and other outputs should be visible, regularly referred to and regularly refreshed, not only pulled out of the bottom drawer once a year.
- The environment, pre-engagement, timing and setting of the meeting should be carefully considered to maximise an open, receptive and constructive outcome.
- If evidence is collected and well documented in advance it is less necessary for both parties to constantly be distracted by the need to take detailed notes 'for HR'. The notes from any meeting should be short, concise and contain any actions or disputed issues.
- Positive endorsement of an achievement or a satisfied client should not wait until the next scheduled review – timely recognition, clearly linked to the achievement and backed up by some public endorsement or, if it fits with the firm's general approach, appropriate reward, is most effective. The tech company NetApp aims to 'catch someone doing something right'[62] and recognise it there and then.
- Be agile in terms of outcomes – be ready to move things around to provide someone with the experience they lack or give them a chance to deepen their skills in an area they shine in.

Overlaid across the new approach should be a recalibration of your people processes from highly individual to team based. There is already a cadre of law firms, from global titans to small start-ups, who have dispensed with individual targets and metrics for chargeable hours or fees in favour of team targets, which the entire team has collective responsibility for. The aim is to dismantle some of the historic impediments to greater collaboration and team working.

I have worked with firms to steadily deconstruct their complete focus on individual performance and replace it with a primarily team-based structure. Moving in that direction is imperative for any firm that wants to stimulate the healthy growth of self-managed, highly collaborative and client-centred teams. This shift requires ambitious but achievable team goals that really inspire and motivate team members. These should not be purely financial. The right place to start is always with client service delivery – identifying measurable and objective benchmarks and being clear about how the data, including client feedback, will be obtained and reported.

When reviewing and evaluating performance, the ideal format to encourage is one where the entire team is together, with a range of data inputs available to them all, and the environment is conducive to all members having an input. When it comes to individual review meetings, your aim is to set some objectives based on how that person can most positively contribute to the team goals and to review their contribution each time. Both team and individual performance cycles should be fully integrated with the Agile model, connecting with the language and structure of your other Agile tools – whether that is LPM, design thinking or Agile features such as sprints, client stories, tasks and backlogs.

6. How Agile teams and project management enhance your human dimension

Implementing a more engaging human dimension in your firm might start when you roll-out an Agile team and project model. The fundamentals of Agile I explored in the first few chapters inevitably bring with them changed working practices that have a direct impact on the individuals in those teams. Major change will always inspire a range of emotional reactions and some of them will be negative, especially in the initial stages. However, there are many positive benefits to your people that adopting Agile methodologies should produce. Your people should be:

- more engaged in and aware of the team's activities;
- consulted, listened to and able to contribute ideas and improvements;
- more skilled and knowledgeable about ways of working, client service tools and technologies;
- directly responsible for positive client outcomes and improvements to the value you offer;
- empowered, with more of a say in their work and their team;

- part of a high-functioning and focused team;
- excited and optimistic about further change and improvement; and
- re-focused on value-adding activity and less bogged-down in administration.

Everyone involved in setting up and overseeing the pilot needs to set out how to achieve these human outcomes from the start and track, adjust and iterate throughout to ensure they are delivered.

> **Agile first steps – human**
> - Revisit your language, style of communication and key HR processes, evaluating whether you are treating employees as adults, customers and human beings.
> - Review your new post-pandemic Agile working guidance and policies to ensure they are founded on a basis of mutual trust and respect.
> - Lead from the front with senior colleagues by adopting servant leadership principles and behaviours.
> - Overhaul your performance management and review processes with an Agile mindset – see "Agile performance management" section above.

VII. Fluid and flexible (workplace and workforce)

1. The legal workplace and workforce reimagined
The workplace and workforce dimensions incorporate the resourcing, organisational design and infrastructure strategy of law firms, where the meaning and usage of that word Agile morphs a little. The core concepts I have already examined remain constant – agility still embodies responsiveness, client-centricity, transparency, a constant pursuit of improvement and innovation. However, in the organisational domain Agile working is used interchangeably with flexible working. This chapter will look at the development of Agile and flexible working thinking in the legal sector and consider the dramatic impact of the 2020 pandemic on an emerging new law firm model.

Agile working represents a major change to the established and once nearly universal law firm business model. The move towards a more Agile model is bound up with the need to achieve great efficiency, responsiveness to peaks and troughs in demand and to minimise waste and unutilised capacity. But there is a strong employee attraction, retention and engagement imperative as well, reflecting a generational shift in our legal workforce and the move to centre-stage of a very different set of staff expectations and needs, as we enter the third decade of the 21st century. The outcome you are aiming for is a new dynamic people model – fluid, empowered, responsive and collaborative.

In creating an Agile approach, you will also unlock an ability to achieve a more diverse and inclusive firm. Many of the most established, fixed and unchallenged foundations of the law firm model combine to build barriers to talented women and people from ethnic and disadvantaged communities. Those include the default graduate/top university recruitment route, cost of legal education, lack of engagement with large parts of the communities firms work within, long working hours, inflexible working hours, presenteeism, narrow performance and promotion evaluation and metrics, eat-what-you-kill remuneration and veneration of tradition. There are many others. Law firms, like most organisations, have also suffered from multiple forms of unconscious bias which react with these entrenched behaviours to limit access and progression. Many firms have focused a lot of attention and energy on diversity and inclusion and there is a widespread determination to address the issue in this generation. To do that, firms will have to challenge and dismantle some of the pillars of the conventional firm model and embrace agility.

One fundamental shift in expectations is the decline in the number of lawyers focused on, or even interested in, making partner in a private practice law firm. Underpinning this shift is the breakdown of career-long attachment and loyalty to one firm, or even to one profession. Alongside that, staff expect more flexibility and less time in the office.

"Contracting out or outsourcing has also been used to enable law firms to extend their hours of service and availability to clients."

For the firm, especially for its senior leadership and HR teams, these shifts can represent a headache, with the conflicting expectations and attitudes of different generations in today's workforce hard to reconcile. Gen Z workers, born after 1995, are entering the workforce in significant numbers now and bringing sharply contrasting ideas from the traditionalist and boomer generations that built the prevailing law firm model and still retain a foothold in the upper echelons of firms. Adapting firmly established approaches to hiring, training, supervision, reward and recognition and career progression can be painful and represents an unfinished 'work-in-progress' in the legal sector.

As well as big changes emerging from inside firms – from its people – parallel upheavals on the supply side have further upset the late 20th-century model. Spurred on by reinvigorated clients looking for more choice and better value, plenty of alternative legal resource models have sprung up over the last two decades. Clients can tap directly into contract attorney or virtual lawyer businesses. They can also decide to outsource the entire matter or block of legal work not to one of their usual law firm providers but to an alternative legal service provider (some of whom began life as 'legal process outsourcing' (LPO) companies) or law company.

Law firms are now adapting their own resourcing model to be more flexible when they need additional resource – sometimes utilising these same alternative, third-party sources or creating their own flexible resourcing models, leveraging alumni or freelancers. Contracting out or outsourcing has also been used to enable law firms to extend their hours of service and availability to clients. In addition, a surge, even pre-pandemic, in interest in part-time, variable-hours and home-working has stimulated the creation of a supplementary, highly qualified additional labour pool.

Utilising more sophisticated resource management tools is more important as the legal workforce becomes more fluid and flexible. There has been a move to develop or buy in tools designed for professional service firms in larger firms where the dividend from bringing more order and structure to this area has been quoted as a 7%+ lift in lawyer utilisation. That figure comes from Dave Cook, a specialist in this arena and developer of the Mason & Cook resource management tools (now part of BigHand). He also highlights the benefits which bring objectivity, data and a real-time view of capacity and allocation bring to the diversity and inclusion and career development agendas. During the pandemic, having a resource management view of your workforce became even more valuable, shining a light on availability and workloads despite everyone working remotely.[63]

There are a high proportion of women in this group, including many returning to legal work after a break for childcare or other reasons, and that is one of a number of positive indicators that the legal sector is now finding a way to include and engage a more diverse talent pool. Alongside this positive trend, further pushing up the proportion of women lawyers (already over 50% in many legal jurisdictions), many firms are beginning to find more innovative ways to reach out to traditionally overlooked communities and demographics when populating intern programmes, training programmes and hiring into other roles. The potential talent mix of the future law firm should become more diverse and inclusive if we can keep up this impetus.

Another notable trend has been the rise of platform or consultant law firms (other labels, more prosaic, are 'distributed' or 'fee-sharing' firms). In the UK legal market, four large players have emerged – Keystone Law, Gunnercooke, Setfords and Taylor Rose. They now employ over 1,000 freelance lawyers. The largest of them, Keystone Law, has floated to become one of the handful of listed legal businesses, and now sits in the UK Top 100 law firms by turnover. Right at the end of 2020, renowned investor newsletter *The Motley Fool* selected Keystone Law as one of the *3 monster growth stocks I'd buy for 2021 and beyond*, noting that the company "currently has over 350 lawyers on its platform yet believes its addressable market is nearly 50,000 lawyers ... I'm quite excited by the disruptive potential here".[64] These models, along with others which have a focus on specific segments, eg female lawyers returning to the workforce, have brought the 'gig economy' into the heart of the legal sector. Lawyers can operate as freelancers with a high degree of autonomy but without the regulatory, financial and employer risk of starting up their own firm. The working practices and attractive 'deal' that has appealed to lawyers joining these firms has, in turn, inspired more flexible arrangements offered by conventional law firms, who now find themselves competing for talent against these very different rivals.

The new dynamic people model in law firms is shaping up to be notably more fluid, empowered, responsive, collaborative and, naturally, agile. Consider the extent to which you have flexed your own model in the following ways:

- flexible working – enabling your people to work wherever, whenever, however is most appropriate and effective for the task in hand;
- flexible resourcing – using alternative sources of legal and other skills to more closely fit resource with workload across the firm;
- redesigned contracting – multiple, flexible variations on the conventional permanent, full time, fixed hours and fixed location contract for employees;

- alternative career structures – new roles, career routes, non-partnership options, breaks and return to work programmes;
- outsourcing and shared service centres – relocating or entirely contracting out parts of the firm, especially to lower cost locations which are not established legal centres;
- achieving genuine diversity and inclusion across the workforce – tapping into previously overlooked or unreached talent pools;
- responding to changing generational expectations and demands in order to attract and retain talent;
- responding to changing client needs, behaviours and expectations by flexing your resourcing and organisational model (eg, by extending availability or providing additional services);
- adapting your firm's Agile organisation design to support and reflect these changes; and
- adapting your firm's physical and virtual infrastructure to support and respond to these changes, including digital/paperless transformation and 'working from anywhere' (WFA).

2. Embracing Hybrid/Agile working

Behind many of these changes are sweeping, era-defining shifts in society, economy and technology. These changes are not unique to the legal sector – they affect every part of our world which is what makes them so powerful, inexorable and irresistible. The legal sector and law firms do not get to decide whether these trends will change our world.

Our experiences in 2020 indicated the sheer power of external influences on driving sudden, dramatic change into the law, at the same time exposing just how changed law firms already were. The ability of firms to respond so promptly and effectively to the pandemic, flipping into digital, remote working mode almost overnight underlined that the intrinsic nature of firms had changed, perhaps without us fully appreciating it, many years ago. Professor Richard Susskind believes that the 2020s will be "the decade when many of the radical tech-led programmes being designed now will really come to life …"[65] and that, looking back, 2016 had been the 'tipping point' year in which he felt the majority of the legal audience as a whole accepted that transformational change was coming and were eager to hear how to deal with it. That is now five years' ago and the underlying changes wrought in our firms have become much more evident. The Hybrid/Agile firm, with a high proportion of its people working from anywhere for a substantial proportion of the week, appears to be the default organisational model and my work with chief operating officers in the Legal COO Network indicates that has already, *de facto*, become a permanent change.

While many partners still tell me that they feel their core values, culture and strategic direction are immutable, the evidence suggests something different – we are mid-way through the biggest reset of the law firm model in decades and the pace of that transition from here onwards will be much faster.

> **Agile toolkit – designing and delivering Hybrid/Agile working**
> I use the compound label *Hybrid/Agile* to describe the transformed working model that not just legal services but most previously office-based industries have adopted at an incredible pace. The two dimensions are equally important in our futures. *Hybrid* emphasises the synthesis of hub office locations and remote working from home or just about anywhere else. *Agile* emphasises that those settings can be deployed and integrated in almost infinitely flexible combinations at short notice to suit the immediate need. And that new locations and working patterns can and will be added to that mix as we progress.
>
> This approach to the legal workforce and workplace is not entirely new and is not simply a knee-jerk response to COVID-19, potentially exposed to a rapid backlash. I opened up our first entirely open-plan, dress-down office with Osborne Clarke way back in 1998. We had taken the whole national firm into open buildings with activity-based working zones by 2004. Many law firm leaders I have spoken to in the last year have been pleased, and relieved, to relay how well prepared they were with their mobile working infrastructure when the pandemic and lockdowns hit. Steve Sumner, IT Director at UK lawyers Taylor Vinters LLP makes the point that most lawyers "were Agile to some extent, travelling to meet clients and working remotely prior to COVID".[66]
>
> Hybrid/Agile working introduces new levels of agility to how you utilise both workforce and workplace. This transformation centres on four dimensions – where people work, how people work, the roles people do, and the time people work.
>
> While a lot of effort has gone into evolving and refining these Hybrid/Agile models since the pandemic and lockdowns first hit, it felt like we were still operating in an extended period of experimentation. This section serves as a whistle-stop tour of some of the biggest issues and ideas that will need to be considered and addressed in order to establish a new normal model that really works for you.
>
> **Hybrid/Agile working – where people work**
> An evolution in the working patterns of lawyers and law firms have been underway since before the turn of the century, as the industry

"As 2020 drew to a close I heard, in survey after survey and on the many calls I chaired with COOs and managing partners, 90% or more of firms report that the move to a Hybrid/Agile way of working would be permanent."

incrementally absorbed and leveraged advances in technology and responded to shifting social trends. How we live, and work, now is very different from how we did 20 years ago. The viability for most of us to work anytime, anyplace, anywhere arrived some time ago. Law firms placed new expectations on their people to be more accessible and productive on the road, when out with clients or at conferences and, increasingly, at home. At the same time, some firms were willing to offer some limited flexibility to employees to work from home and flex their hours.

In 2020 COVID-19 acted as an unforeseen and explosive accelerant to these trends. Some firms responded by closing down offices and shifting to nearly 100% remote working for an extended period. Others found it impossible to work effectively on a fully remote basis but managed to limit numbers in the office at any one time and redesign the workspace to manage through the long COVID period with a Hybrid 'make-do' approach. As 2020 drew to a close I heard, in survey after survey and on the many calls I chaired with COOs and managing partners, 90% or more of firms report that the move to a Hybrid/Agile way of working would be permanent. Almost nobody intended to return to primarily office-based working and the majority predicted that staff would, on average, work from home up to 50% of the time.

The unprecedented challenges posed by the pandemic have made agility, already an ambition for many firms, an operational imperative. Many firms would agree they experienced more change in a matter of months in 2020 than they had over the previous 10 years. But that change process was visceral, incredibly fast and reactive. Over the next few years, you are having to make big bets on the medium to long term and on what the more permanent reshaped ways of working will look like. In many ways this will be more difficult and involve judgements and balances you have few precedents for. In early 2021 a Williams Lea/Sandpiper survey of over 400 legal respondents revealed that employee engagement and well-being issues were now deemed the greatest challenges for firms to address.[67] The two lists of hot button issues below highlight just how tough balancing the benefits (the first list) and disadvantages (the second list) of the Hybrid/Agile working model will be. The cover of *The Economist* on 10 September 2020 summed up the high stakes involved – it read, "Office Politics: The fight over the future of work".[68]

Hot button opportunities for designing *where* people work include:

- retaining productivity gains reported by many firms from pandemic remote working – how to keep the efficiency, punctuality and collaboration between teams in multiple locations;
- eliminating/reducing commuting and travel down-time;
- the ability to manage domestic and work commitments flexibly and smartly;
- completing digitisation of all areas of your business;
- extended hours coverage;
- the ability to hire talent from anywhere;
- losing restrictions on existing employee location – don't have to leave if they relocate, aren't likely to leave due to commute;
- meeting and communication efficiency, punctuality and effectiveness;
- stimulating evolution of much better digital collaboration and communication tools;
- echoing clients own digital and virtual journeys and meeting their demand for new ways of working;
- clients no longer wanting to be dictated to or told "you will come to our offices, we only work on these days and within these hours, you can only contact us or pay us etc this way";
- satellites, more localised hub and serviced offices that bridge the gap between big city-centre offices and home working – with potential benefits for both client/new business and staff;
- working from anywhere benefits for those with second homes, family or other carer duties that take them away, a partner who works to a very different schedule (eg, a teacher) etc;

- real-estate savings – the opportunity to scale back the fixed, lavish and expensive big city office locations with underutilised partitioned offices for the lawyers; and
- reinventing the office as somewhere people are magnetically drawn to and want to 'use' for specific purposes (eg, collaboration, client engagement) rather than required to attend.

Hot button issues and threats for designing *where* people work include:

- loss of control and big challenges to supervision;
- the exposure of issues of trust between managers/supervisors and their teams;
- generational (and seniority) and office/home worker conflict – the more senior people are often better set-up for home working and less inclined to spend as much time in the office in the future, while younger more junior staff may feel they are obliged to do so;
- infrastructure – offices, technology and home-working set-up – is often not fit for purpose in a Hybrid/Agile world;
- large professional businesses who have a privileged position perceived to have abandoned cities, their real estate largely dormant, not supporting the local supply chain;
- city centres and offices lack attraction for staff – less busy and buzzy and with fewer retail, food and drink outlets etc;
- lack of genuine support for home working – financial, equipment, adjusted expectations and working hours etc;
- cultural, financial and habitual attachment to office working and fear of the unknown;
- onboarding, mentoring and training new hires;
- team working effectiveness, especially the collegiate 'buzz' of working as a team in a physical environment;
- ensuring sporadic office attendance does not become random – connecting people, communicating availability and planning forward;
- mental health and loneliness, especially for younger workers, urban dwellers, extroverts;
- collaboration, serendipity and the watercooler moment;
- lacking seamless connectivity and availability to client and colleagues for home and mobile workers;
- hot-desking – virus prevention, dislike of administrative elements (eg, desk booking);
- Zoom fatigue and unexplored side-effects of extended isolated, home working;
- erosion of protected 'home' space and time ('we aren't working at home, we are living in the office');

- some clients – elders, those with big emotional issues they want to talk about personally, digitally disadvantaged – want a more traditional, in-person or paper-based service (though the proportion is dropping and many of them now want both in-person and digital options); and
- interruptions, disruptions and even planned and scheduled non-work duties disturbs the home working day, unlike office working.

Hybrid/Agile working – how people work
The ability to work from home or from different offices has become the norm in most professional firms, large and small. But do you have flexibility within the workplace itself? Do you have breakout areas where staff can have informal meetings and discuss ideas? Is there WiFi throughout the building that convert every piece of floorspace into effective infrastructure? Are you enabling your people to work in whatever way suits them best and makes them most productive?

This period saw more changes than simply the relocation of most workers from office to home. Increased virtuality dominated every part of our working lives. Lawyers, banks and other professionals

"The ability to work from home or from different offices has become the norm in most professional firms, large and small."

completed big deals end-to-end without anyone meeting in person. The ingrained habit of business travel for meetings, conferences, interviews and networking became something we could only dimly recall – aspects of it much missed, others not so much. Our communication with clients, contacts and co-workers shifted from a mix of in-person and phone to primarily video based. Paper, for long the target of a 'paperlite' campaign to persuade reluctant old-school lawyers to ditch the files and embrace full digital working, was thrown sharply into relief – it was indeed the Achilles' heel of law firm operations. The individuals, teams and practice areas that had remained most reliant on paper found it hardest to thrive not just in the pandemic period itself but in a post-pandemic new digitised world. One of the other biggest discoveries triggered by enforced home working for lawyers and their teams has been the recognition that, in a highly digital world, the level of secretarial support provided exceeded demand. A series of large firm support staff redundancy announcements have followed. The full embrace of digital working by these large firms will flow through all tiers of the legal market and support staff numbers in small to mid-sized firms will fall dramatically over the next few years. In a recent survey of law firms in the United Kingdom and the United States respondents expected 58% of their current secretaries to have left the firm, due to retirement or job losses, in the next five years.[69]

Hot buttons for designing *how* people work include:

- activity-based working – matching the working environment and fit-out to the task(s) people need to do, rather than a 'one-size-fits-all' conventional, fixed workstation or office;
- matching working environment to personality – designing to suit, eg, extrovert and introvert personality types;
- client areas designed to deliver on your brand promise;
- space for innovation and collaboration – suited to the Agile team structure;
- real-estate planning and reduction – driven by 'compelling events', eg, COVID-19;
- unallocated desking and seamless working inside the office – making it easy to find and book space to work when people do come into the office;
- true mobility – constantly testing and refining the infrastructure that maintains the same high quality of work setting anytime, anyplace, anywhere;
- cyber security and managing the risk of switching locations and working on the move;
- captives and shared service centres – onshore and offshore shared service centres that can be designed very differently from offices that operate as collaboration and client meeting

hubs, but need to reflect the firm's employer brand and promise of a great place to work;
- true distributed or 'virtual' firm models (eg, Keystone Law) – hybrid models that encompass not just employed staff in teams but also solo or small group consultants/gig workers;
- opening 'pop-up' offices in new locations – previously seen as sub-scale, slimmed down new offices can be easily stood-up in new locations at minimal cost to establish a hub, touchdown space or bridge-head into a new market; and
- working in transit – making it easier and more secure.

Hybrid/Agile – the roles people do
Are your people working flexibly enough for you to get the most out of their talents? Often, staff remain focused in a particular area of specialism when they have more to offer, because the organisation has no flexibility to accommodate a change. For example, secondments and job rotation could create a wide pool of skills that could be deployed to meet temporary or periodic demands in certain areas.

Hot buttons for designing the *roles* people do include:

- AI, automation and the implication for jobs – determining the right mix of human labour and digital labour for each part of your firm;
- new organisation design – breaking down silos and encouraging multi-disciplinary teams;
- broadening practice group management out from a single head to 'cabinet style' management team with delegated responsibilities and input from other business professionals;
- the essential skills your 'digital lawyers' will need in the 2020s;
- sector-based roles – structuring some roles around key clients or sectors, rather than only around practice groups and legal discipline;
- consolidated, national and international practice groups and roles;
- reflecting the new job types emerging in Agile law firms – examples include legal engineer, legal project management, analyst and many more;
- centralised shared resource – in areas like project management, procurement, document production (DP), LPM, process improvement, PMO, applied technology;
- in-house and outsourced roles – focusing your employed workforce on core competencies, client-value delivery and work you are confident your firm can do better, cheaper, faster than third parties;
- captives and shared service centres – reviewing the

organisation design and roles used in the highly effective shared service centres run by large law firms as well as by corporates: what can you learn and deploy in your own firm?
- how you recruit – simply turning to agencies to find full-time, permanent hires is no longer the only, or best, option to secure talent. Your talent acquisition mix can include crowdsourcing part time or freelance staff, bringing retirees in on short-term projects, tapping into alumni or volunteers, apprenticeships or partnerships with other organisations; and
- reinventing the mix of early career stage roles – utilising apprenticeship, programmes for diverse and disadvantaged communities, new model internships alongside the conventional trainee lawyer intake.

Hybrid/Agile – the time people work
Flexible approaches to working hours have become common. But beyond part-time working or 'glide time' hours, think too about whether some roles can have annualised hours? Whether you can flex the workforce according to seasonal, or other variable demands? Can you flex hours and terms to suit your workforce better, including working parents and home workers, and boost retention and attraction of key talent?

Two of the most challenging implications of the widespread move to working from home we saw in 2020 fall into this category. We are experiencing a dramatic rise in the number of women leaving the overall workforce as a direct consequence of the pandemic period and in law many of them are highly qualified lawyers. The burdens of parenting and working from home over an extended period seem to have been 'the last straw' for many. The same period has seen us take another step towards entirely dissolving the barriers between private/domestic and work time. Many firms report their people working longer hours and working evenings and weekends interchangeably with weekdays. The new ways of working provide positive flexibility benefits but the price in terms of overwork, erosion of personal life and burn-out looks too high unless we make some changes.

Hot buttons for re-designing the *time* people work include:

- flexible hours contracts and best practices;
- creative alternatives to redundancy and entirely losing talent and experience;
- secretarial and PA staffing redesign – especially in the wake of lawyers learning new levels of self-sufficiency while home working in 2020;
- gig economy, flex lawyer and zero hours contracts;

- flexible benefits schemes;
- seasonal contracts (used for example by tax firms who have peak resourcing around tax year end);
- the negative impact of working from home on particular groups, including parents, women and ethnic minorities;
- real-estate utilisation – shifts, overlapping hours, alternative uses in evening/weekends ('sweating the asset');
- personal security and supervision issues arising from extended hours and home working;
- tailoring work patterns to domestic and family commitments;
- planned wind-down or alternative routes to retirement for partners and staff;
- flexible shift patterns and location choices to support international firms with 'follow-the-sun' services.

Agile first steps – fluid and flexible
- Crystallise and confirm your 2020s Hybrid/Agile working model addressing and balancing the multiple hot button issues identified in this chapter.
- Deliver at least three significant improvements to your people's remote/home/mobile working experience each year.
- Rethink, redesign and reshape your office real-estate portfolio.
- Identify areas where use of contract, freelance, business partner and 'as a service' resourcing can replace full-time employed defaults to increase agility.
- Dismantle or defuse the institutional barriers to greater diversity and inclusion – see the beginning of this chapter for a list.

VIII. Organically collaborative

1. Network and platform organisations
Placing small highly autonomous teams at the heart of the Agile model could suggest an acceptance of teams going their own way and not being bound into the whole. Agile organisations absolutely do not work this way. Collaboration and connectivity are preconditions of success in these firms, but very fast horizontal communications are far more important than the conventional vertical consultations and approvals.

Each team is able to manage itself towards its own goals but at the same time understands its place within, and responsibilities to, the wider firm. Teams are interdependent, rather than independent. They form a network or ecosystem. They do not stand alone (as I suspect they do not in your organisation today; though you might question how much thought and effort has gone into describing and defining how connections between your teams work).

One thing that binds teams together is a shared common purpose. I will explore that further when we look at the 10th and final Agile Attribute. They should also be set up with connecting routines and processes that make it easy for them to, first, support each other in overcoming their challenges and, second, learn from each other.

An additional layer of complexity has been added to the task of creating a highly effective network model since spring 2020 as many organisations reconcile themselves to the nodes of that network being increasingly individuals, rather than teams, and working in a multitude of highly distributed, remote locations.

Perhaps the most important single example of highly collaborative Agile organisation structures in our lifetime is Apple who developed a relatively simple hardware device – the iPhone – in an iterative fashion and then offered up a platform to mobilise independent software developers. Hundreds of thousands of small teams of developers contributed their ingenuity and talents to build apps in an iterative fashion while interacting directly with customers. The car is now following this trajectory. The engineering output of the factory – the vehicle itself – is no longer static but constantly being developed and enhanced by collaborative software and upgrades, long after the customer has taken delivery and begun driving it.

Almost all organisations, and this is certainly true of law firms, simply will not have all the right skills and infrastructure to deliver the full product and service experience their clients, corporations and individuals will increasingly demand. This requires a collaborative

"There are alternative ways of growing your firm in the areas you really need to without the lottery of lateral hiring, but these alternative collaborative models may only be open to firms with the Agile mindset."

model, where partnering with other complementary service providers, with your clients themselves and with smart, disruptive start-ups is an essential part of the formula. As with the Apple example, the platform model has begun to take a hold in multiple industries. In legal itself, Reynen Court[70] has arrived on the scene in the last few years – a collaborative venture between a cluster of law firms and tech companies. Leading software conglomerate, Thomson Reuters, have unveiled their Panoramic[71] platform which wraps up a series of their leading legal applications. Law firms like Dentons, Hogan Lovells and Norton Rose have taken the Swiss Verein and other organisational collaboration structures and built ever-expanding empires of co-branded but institutionally independent law firms across the globe.

2. Collaborate to grow – the Agile growth strategy
Organic growth in law firms has been predicated on sometimes aggressive lateral hiring of partners. This attempts to lock in big-ticket new hires via a game of escalating promises and expectations. Study after study has exposed the high failure-rate of laterals and there is a diaspora of partners who now hop from firm to firm every few years, proving the continued triumph of hope over experience. At the same time, large firms have been getting larger through acquisition. The scale economics these acquisitions tap into are very powerful and have produced a growing gap between top-tier global firms and the next group, often in terms of profitability as well as revenues. But these complete firm acquisitions generally involve taking on a lot of headcount and cost that was not core to the original aim – years of integration effort, cleaning up problem practices, testing and ultimately parting company with partners who aren't performing or don't fit. There are alternative ways of growing your firm in the areas you really need to without the lottery of lateral hiring, but these alternative collaborative models may only be open to firms with the Agile mindset.

An Agile growth strategy still starts with the ambitions and aims you want your firm to achieve in terms of extended and improved client service and the resulting scale and financial outcomes. You will still need to identify capability and resource gaps you want to address. The difference comes in terms of the range of routes you evaluate in order to achieve your goal. At the heart of the Agile growth strategy is the inclusion of collaborative options that sit beyond the assumption that expanding the scope and scale of your client service offering can only be done via a wholly owned or employed route. I will highlight four collaborative routes that address a strategic growth goal without relying on the permanent, risky and expensive lateral hiring or acquisition defaults:

- *Create a joint venture with one, or more, other businesses that extends the range of services to your existing client and contact base.* Your partner could be another law firm or a provider of other professional services (or it could be, for example, a tech company joint venturing around a legal tech product) with complementary capabilities to your own. Your partner has the capabilities and you have the clients – a successful joint venture will allow your firm to both meet your clients' needs and earn a share of the new revenues that you were previously unable to tap. Your partner will deliver profitable services to a client-base they are currently unable to easily access.
- *Collaborate to extend the 'reach' and market for your existing services.* This alternative puts you in the shoes of the partner in the first option. In this case you have deep and market-leading capabilities in one or more area that you have not been able to leverage in a much wider market – extending, say, to larger businesses, new sectors or a new geography. Your partner has reputation and clients in those markets and, ideally, some adjacent service offerings that provide you with the opportunity to go to market together. In an ideal scenario, you have a series of complementary capabilities that deliver a succession of win/win opportunities for your joint venture.
- *Create a long-term Agile business combination.* Standard-issue law firm mergers and acquisitions and lateral hires are themselves long-term business combinations. Some big differences between those and Agile approaches relate to term, branding and control. Firms are going to have more options in an Agile world to flex and fit the terms of any deal more precisely to their needs.

Taking term, or permanence, first. Fear of the huge leap that joining permanently with another firm through merger represents one of the biggest drags on legal market consolidation. Partners know they are committing themselves and their firm to a change that is a gamble – very public and difficult to reverse or refine. Agile collaboration offers a long-term, but not permanent, commitment – enough to deliver on the strategic potential and yield a return on investment but with a clear, mutual escape route or renewal date. Technology and the fluid, flexible resourcing options now available have combined to enable organisations to work together 'as one', without making an eternal commitment to each other in every dimension.

Legal brand management is developing fast. We have seen an emerging model of a legal 'portfolio of brands' in the last few years; not, of course, a new concept in the corporate world, where it is conventional wisdom to acquire companies and retain their name and brand, building a stable of different but complementary brands. In the legal world, the default established over decades is that common branding and the

"Fear of the huge leap that joining permanently with another firm through merger represents one of the biggest drags on legal market consolidation."

building of a single, big, consolidated firm is the right route. The massive growth of the largest global law brands has used institutional vehicles such as the Swiss Verein to enable networks of legally separate firms around the globe to be co-branded and presented as huge single, seamless global firms. This is a tactic already honed by the Big 4 accounting firms. Agile thinking in the legal market is now questioning this default. Some acquisitive and ambitious firms or investors see the potential to build a group of legal service brands under common ownership, leveraging funding, technology and central support but allowing the individual brands to continue to build their reputation and client base. This could be an attractive option for firms and a successful, alternative strategy for the consolidators. In the United Kingdom, mid-tier firm Shakespeare Martineau announced in 2020 its 'House of Brands' strategy as follows:

> *proactively seeking mergers, acquisitions, team recruitment and lateral hires – but with a difference. Shakespeare Martineau is becoming a 'house of brands' group with the mindset that each brand will be able to 'have their cake and eat it' as the structure offers other firms an alternative route to growth.*[72]

Finally, control. This is emotionally connected to brand in the minds of many firms contemplating the prospect of being acquired or joining a much larger entity. The current assumption is that they will probably have to lose *both* brand and control, perhaps after a few years' grace period. The two do not necessarily need to be coupled in this way, however, and there are options for groups of partners/owners in a legal business to join a larger entity without ceding all control and autonomy. Don't forget that self-management and getting the decisions made closer to the client are fundamentals of Agile. If firms in a new city or region or which add new practice areas are being acquired, the current leaders of those firms can retain a greater degree of control over their remit than previously. This enables those leaders to continue to have a significant say in how services are delivered and developed, while still tapping into and utilising the powerful synergies and shared services of the bigger organisation. It is good to see more acquirers in the legal market present this as their approach, which represents an alternative to the assumption that control and decision making needs to be centralised and wielded further away from the ultimate client as firms get larger.

- One other long-standing collaboration route offers an interesting option in an Agile world. Many firms continue to find just the right balance – of scale synergies and independent control, big brand marketing and niche or local proposition – from membership of a strong legal or professional services network. Increasingly, the big global networks like Lex Mundi have positioned themselves up as a direct alternative to joining a large unified global legal brand like Dentons, Norton Rose Fulbright or Baker McKenzie. Member firms, generally top-rated in their jurisdictions, have the option to retain independence and their own brand, while joining together with like-minded firms for knowledge sharing, collaborative projects and client referrals. At a national level, multi-firm networks like LawNet in the United Kingdom have continued to expand and develop closer ties between members through the 'age of consolidation' – demonstrating law firm enthusiasm for collaborative and Agile alternatives to merger and acquisition.

There are a host of structural, competition and branding questions to resolve once you get beneath the surface of any of these options. The contractual, organisational/entity, legal, risk, financial and brand dimensions of any joint venture involve some big questions. But not necessarily on the scale of those issues which arise from a full-scale acquisition or merger, or from a prolonged campaign of senior later hires. We are simply more used to those approaches. They seemed like the right solutions in a less Agile, apparently more predictable world – even though they probably failed as often as they succeeded.

The collaborative route can also allow many more firms to extend their offering further than just legal advice. This is something we have already seen happen in the dynamic ALSP market – with Simmons & Simmons acquiring Wavelength, EY acquiring Riverview Law and Elevate acquiring a whole series of diverse alternative legal businesses. Partnering and joint ventures opens up to the wider market – not just the Big 4 – the much-discussed combination of legal and accounting services for example. By extending their strategic horizons beyond what can be achieved just through lateral hiring and law firm merger and acquisition, firms have far more opportunities than they appreciated to develop new value-adding services for clients and to find more clients who need their existing expertise, without the poison-pill of inevitably having to lose their autonomy and a brand developed over decades in the process.

In a more Agile world and provided your firm has the Agile mindset, the range of vehicles and collaborative structures you can utilise expands. As more firms use the kinds of joint ventures we have seen, for example, between law firms and insurers in the United Kingdom, where joint venture alternative business structures have become common, or between technology companies and law firms in the emerging legal tech arena, the number of variations on these models will become more numerous.

Agile first steps – organically collaborative
- Ask every team and team leader to identify three teams they currently collaborate closely with and at least three more they will collaborate more closely with to deliver value next year.
- Ask a multi-disciplinary team to review the opportunities for building out a product or service platform model to deliver extended value to both your clients and the firm.
- Run a strategic analysis of the best third-party collaboration options and models for achieving growth through extending your offer and/or market over the next decade – use Agile ideation principles here and generate lots of ideas, however fanciful, and gradually focus on a core set of your best options.

IX. Restless, radical and challenging

1. Strategic agility

A large amount of this report focuses its attention on what Steven Denning calls operational agility.[73] That is not intended to demean the transformative effort required to take what you do and how you do it and overhaul things.

Embracing an Agile mindset at every level of your firm will, however, engage another form of Agile activity – strategic agility. Exemplified by an Apple or Amazon, this is the state of constantly looking for, identifying and then delivering market-creating innovation. Innovation is aimed at creating new products and services or entirely new markets that your firm, or law firms generally, have not previously had. Or going further and transforming the very core of your firm, reinventing your business model – like Netflix did in switching from an online DVD library into a streaming and content creation giant.

The idea of obsessively looking to create new markets felt very alien to legal services until recently. But a shift has begun. There are three essential ways in which a firm can liberate its mindset and embrace strategic agility, ready for market-creating innovation. Your thinking will redirect from existing products and services to potential new products and services; from existing clients to future clients; and, finally, from seeing your business as a 'law firm', providing legal advice delivered by lawyers, to one that can take any number of routes to facilitate the outcomes your clients are looking for.

This shift in perception has not come to the wider legal market yet. Most law firms are still comfortable offering a predictable and restricted set of services delivered in a conventional way to the same clients or type of clients. However, there are some legal sector developments that demonstrate the kind of radical Agile thinking this chapter is all about. Examples include:

- the creation of alternative legal service provider subsidiaries and legal tech divisions by large law firms;
- tech applications being developed and launched which offer new digital, often more efficient routes for clients to resolve legal issues;
- creation of powerful multi-disciplinary service firms, especially but not exclusively by the Big 4 accounting firms, to offer clients a hybrid service incorporating legal components;
- entirely new, low or no cost solutions that address the massive latent legal market where potential clients have typically been reluctant to turn to traditional law firms;
- digital do-it-yourself solutions for legal documents or legal advice; and
- emerging multi-provider platforms (including Reynen Court, Thomson Reuters' Panoramic) that offer legal customers a new seamless and integrated suite of applications.

These examples, and there are many others, highlight the strategic unravelling of a once monolithic legal service delivery model is well underway. The ingenuity of business and incredible speed of technology development will, in my view, outpace lawyer protection and undermine large parts of 'practice of law' protection over this decade.

A 2016 PwC report, *The Future of Industries: Bringing Down the Walls*, documents how the boundaries between sectors are dissolving:

> *Technological change is creating historic shifts in industry footprints. Over the next ten years, we think this process will accelerate. Traditional industry classifications will need to be rewritten. Where industry boundaries begin, where they end and who are the main players will all be up for grabs in a number of sectors.*[74]

The boundaries of the legal sector that seemed fixed for all time in the last century feel very fluid today.

"Most law firms are still comfortable offering a predictable and restricted set of services delivered in a conventional way to the same clients or type of clients."

Many of the world's largest law firms are now showing all the signs of 'if you can't beat them, join them' thinking – creating alternative service vehicles and tech products in-house, as well as collaborating with third parties and technology companies. They are well on the way to the next stage of having to accept and adapt to the cannibalisation of some of their most established and previously profitable practices. There is a dawning realisation that if they do not offer to reinvent and replace these practices themselves someone else will do it, soon.

Law firms are having to get strategically Agile and are showing signs that they know this. The first question is whether they can do it well. A second question, given the investment and energy required to create new markets, is whether your firm can exploit the opportunity or idea at scale.

Agile toolkit – Lean Start-Up
The Lean Start-Up idea, popularised by Erie Ries in his 2011 book of the same name,[75] has provided a template for a new generation of entrepreneurs. By folding in the principles of Agile with tools borrowed from Lean and other methodologies, and plenty of lessons learned from real-life start-up experiences, this approach provides a guide not just to entrepreneurs starting up from scratch but to established businesses looking to diversify, reinvent and

launch new products and services. I believe it will emerge as one of the most important frameworks for the legal industry in the 2020s.

Ries insists that we eliminate unchallenged assumptions, gut-feel, 'politics', 'vanity metrics' (he would recognise the law firm focus on rising fee income or recorded hours) and confirmation bias – the tendency to search for and favour information in a way that confirms or supports your own beliefs or values. That may already sound like a tall-order in your firm but please do read on!

In common with many other Agile tools, Lean Start-Up thinking puts the focus squarely on discovering and acting on the client's true needs. It underlines that we should never be satisfied simply with what clients say they want or what we think they want. The approach incorporates many of the same ideas as the information/insight/impact model introduced earlier in the report, pushing advocates to become insight driven organisations.

At the core of Lean Start-Up is the *Build-Measure-Learn* feedback loop. In common with Agile principles, speed is critical – you should aim to enter the Build phase as quickly as possible with a minimum viable product (MVP). The MVP is that version of the product that enables you to complete the Build-Measure-Learn loop in full – getting out and engaging with clients and sourcing their feedback, but with the minimum amount of effort and development time. The antithesis of Lean Start-Up is running a long, detailed pre-planning phase before any new feature, product or service gets produced or anywhere near the client.

In common with the information/insight/impact model, Build-Measure-Learn is, in fact, a cycle. Lean Start-Up also works most effectively in reverse: first, figure out what we need to learn, then what we need to measure to know – *validated learning*. Only then use that learning to figure out what product we need to build and test.

Extending that use of scientific experimental concepts, the *value hypothesis* tests whether a product or service really delivers value to clients once they are using it. Taking any client service, you should set out with a clear baseline metric, an idea about what will improve that metric – the value hypothesis, and a set of experiments designed to test that hypothesis, based around improvements or innovative new features. Lean Start-Up challenges you to eliminate, or at least minimise, time and effort spent on improvement or development that you do not *learn* from. That is an interesting challenge to put to your people working on improvements, innovation, IT and change today.

"Lean Start-Up challenges you to eliminate, or at least minimise, time and effort spent on improvement or development that you do not learn from."

Taking a first step should not be a big problem in law firms – there is plenty of valuable client feedback and input that should be feeding into the backlog of client stories and potential improvements that can be developed and tested. Yet I often hear from frustrated law firm leaders and C-suite executives that there are very few good ideas in their firm and that their lawyers are uncomfortable changing anything. Maybe your firm does not have a flow of new ideas being submitted by your staff, but you are sitting on a reservoir of client issues to work on. Every complaint, response to feedback surveys, query triggered by your bills, prospective client that doesn't proceed after your quote, existing client lost and frustrated outburst from a lawyer about the tools they have to do their job could feed into the service innovation and improvement cycle. Any positive comments and thanks can feed in too, of course. You can turn to these often-untapped sources before you initiate new efforts to engage more regularly and directly with clients or stimulate ideation among our employees.

Is your firm ready to be more flexible about giving time and priority to collating, analysing and then acting on these kinds of insights? That requires a clear message that these are not 'non-value adding' activities just because they are not billable. Starting with a clear message that end of matter reviews should always be conducted and then followed up would be a good first step. Lean Start-Up incorporates the concept of Innovation Accounting – where the most important tracking of value in the organisation measures the accumulation and resolution of learning from client service experiments and iterations. That feels very alien to the legal sector and Eric Ries would point out that we are being blinded by "vanity metrics"[76] – we are valuing and reporting on the wrong things, like many of the established businesses undone by market disruption in the last few decades.

The pivot

Perhaps the best-known part of the Lean Start-Up approach is the pivot. Pivot was the 'word of 2020',[77] thanks to its use, and overuse, to describe every variation of sudden shift in business strategy and channel as a result of the COVID-19 pandemic. In sectors like hospitality, leisure, retail and media the pivot was unavoidable. The most common pivot was from physical and social delivery channels to virtual but there were multiple other ways in which businesses seized opportunities or responded to threats – from manufacturers switching almost overnight to producing personal protective enquipment (PPE) to movie studios moving to launching new films on streaming services.

"Perhaps the best-known part of the Lean Start-Up approach is the pivot."

That word pivot means to change course with one foot anchored to the ground. The last bit is important – this is not a wholesale or random change of direction – your firm or division keeps one foot rooted in what you have done and learned in the past. But it is strategically significant and represents a course correction.

In Lean Start-Up terms, the pivot is the outcome of testing a major new hypothesis about a product or service. The decision about whether to pivot or persevere is integral to the lifecycle of a start-up, or of any new product launch or diversification. It is not evidence of failure, nor a strategic retreat. It is normal and positive – done well it will be the making of your business. However, it is nevertheless a big and inevitably difficult decision and there is a limit to how many times any start-up or other business will want to pivot.

I worry that law firms, and the practice groups that make them up, do not pivot, by and large. And this is a problem. It is many years since the ideas of Harvard's Clayton Christenson and others on disruptive innovation[78] highlighted just how costly – indeed fatal – the failure of market leaders to pivot could be. Their names are now universally recognised as cautionary tales: Blockbuster, Kodak, Barnes & Noble, Sears. Christenson outlined the trajectory of new entrant market disruptors – from them initially being ignored and dismissed by the incumbent market leaders, then establishing a strong foothold in the price-sensitive mid-market and, finally, the market being turned on its head and the established market leaders toppled.

The idea of shifting direction and trying a new approach to a particular service or product, based on a hypothesis, however well informed, sounds inimical to the conservative, risk-averse law firm culture. We are already in an era of accelerating law firm innovation and diversification, but these are seldom about shifting the core business or client base. They are not pivots. But, during a short period in 2020, multiple firms made dramatic shifts in their business models and switched to delivering legal services in a very different way. This transformation was often very rapid and generally highly successful. I think the 2020 experience should provide us with confidence that the legal sector is not implacably hostile territory for the pivot, even though what most of us experienced was not precisely a pivot – a course correction based on a strong client-based hypothesis. It was a necessary, pretty much enforced response to external events that was shared by almost the entire industry and viewed initially as a temporary, rather than sustained, expedient.

There are many ways in which a business, or one strand of it, can pivot. These include:

- zooming-in – on a single, critical and popular feature of a product or service, which then becomes the whole product;
- zooming-out – so that what was the product is integrated as a feature of a much larger product;
- shift segment – when the target client market which the product actually appeals to turns out to be different from the original plan;
- shift client need – we learn that the client need we were trying to solve is not as important as something else which we have the ability to address, we switch to this;
- platformisation – what began as an app is expanded into a platform for clients, containing multiple applications;
- shift business model – based on client responses we identify that we need to shift from high volume, low margin to low volume, high margin or vice versa;
- monetisation – we pivot from one assumed approach to making money from our product to another (in legal terms this could be from a fixed fee per unit to an annual subscription or vice versa, for example);
- channel – a common pivot example for start-ups and new product launches is a shift in the distribution channel – direct/via an agent or intermediary; physical/virtual etc; and
- technology – a complete shift in the tech that enables the product or service.

That is only a sample and brief description of potential pivot options but I think it demonstrates how many alternatives there are for law firms to consider once they open themselves up to the question of whether *to pivot or persevere*.

Agile toolkit – the Five Whys
Fundamental to the Lean Start-Up approach, as well as other Agile tools I have featured in the report, is the use of the Five Whys. This is a well-established, well-known technique, originally popularised as part of the Toyota Production System. The method is deceptively simple but not always easy to adhere to, and capable of producing great results.

Repeating "why" five times in response to a problem can uncover the root cause of the problem and also the solution that will rectify it. This technique enables Lean Start-Up's obsessive search for the 'truth' of client needs and experiences. By continuing to dig deeper, beyond the initial, apparent cause of a problem, we unpeel the layers to get at the actual source.

I mentioned that following the Five Whys can be tough, despite its simplicity. We are all attuned to favour solutions which fit our in-built assumptions and biases, and these often emerge quickly in response to the first and second Whys. It is psychologically hard for people to continue to probe once they have the answer they expected, and five layers of investigation can quickly feel laborious and unlikely to add value.

In the law firm environment, we might be probing client complaints, concerns and issues with our service or internal service failures. Another reason the Five Whys and any similar analytical models can be unpopular is that firms simply lack the data to answer the questions – if you don't spend enough time truly understanding the client's experiences or care enough about what you find, your firm will not have the answers at your fingertips to the Five Whys. Nevertheless, introducing this technique is an easy first step to take. I recently worked with a firm that was part of a large network of independent law firms. The network had, impressively it seemed to me, advocated that all members begin to use the Five Whys as a standard for investigating and documenting client complaints and potential regulatory breaches. There was a concerned response from member firms that this was bureaucratic and overkill when lawyers had so many more important (no doubt billable) things to be doing, despite the opportunity to use a simple tool to start to really uncover the causes of client dissatisfaction and lawyer error.

There is a corollary to the use of techniques such as the Five Whys. That relates to blame and mistakes. Any firm which begins to take a much more forensic (or, the word I have used a few times above, 'obsessive') interest in what clients think about your service and what lies behind complaints and issues, runs the risk of scaring the horses. A determination to get to the bottom of service issues and resolve them can look to some like a witch-hunt. So, it is important to set out your stall about mistakes and blame. First, recognise and communicate the simple fact that it is often failings in the system, not in people, that causes issues – as so many Five Why exercises reveal. Second, make it crystal clear that your approach is to tolerate mistakes the first time they happen. But your aim is to prevent the same mistake from being made twice. That last part is a high bar for any organisation, but take a look at the compliance breach registers and client complaint logs of most law firms and you will see the same issues time and again – repeated for years, never truly resolved and often seen as unavoidable.

2. The competitive imperative

We are witnessing a 'perfect storm' moment for dramatic change and digital transformation that is fuelling new business models for law firms, who are able to redesign themselves in a myriad of ways to meet their future needs. The restless, radical and challenging attribute of Agile law firms achieves its ultimate expression in the ability to review and revise your fundamental structure and business model.

The emergence of a constellation of different types of alternative legal service provider (ALSP) has been a prominent feature of the last decade. As Derek Southall, legal tech and innovation guru and founder of Hyperscale Group, put it when I interviewed him for this report, "there's some very, very well capitalised and tech savvy players coming into the legal sector now". While that was, initially, more obvious in markets like the United Kingdom and Australia, where external capital was able to invest in legal services, it is now very evident that in the United States, by far the world's largest legal market, new entrants are able to begin to chip away at the edges of what was previously uncontested law firm domain, working around the remaining regulatory protection lawyers enjoy. At the same time, I expect we will drop the 'alternative' tag soon as more of the smartest and most progressive established law firms reinventing and rebranding themselves to the extent that they are indistinguishable from the best, most dynamic of the 'alternatives'.

The world we are now entering will not have these artificial divisions that assume a particular type of legal provider has to operate in a particular way. So, you should take an open-minded close look at the ALSP world and what your firm can learn from it. If the Agile law firm means anything it has to mean opening up the firm mindset and identifying, evaluating, trialling and launching new and different ways of delivering value to your clients. One approach to this is to examine how the ALSPs are doing this.

The ALSP has undergone a transition in the last five years. Many of the smaller providers, especially those with a heavy dependence on labour rate arbitrage using offshore employees, have gone to the wall or refocused on other industries that have fewer qualitative and linguistic hurdles to overcome than legal. Meantime, the onshore-based industry has boomed, in the United States, United Kingdom, Australia and, increasingly, across the globe. Providers that initially began as defined legal process outsourcers or contract attorney shops or technology and process improvement houses have integrated and morphed into larger, broad-based businesses that combine the people, process and technology elements together.

ALSPs have been bought and integrated into private equity portfolios and Big 4 accounting firms (EY have acquired both the Thomson Reuters-owned former Pangea3 LPO business and UK-based Riverview Law). Consolidators have emerged from their ranks too – Elevate Services have acquired multiple legal service providers, consultancies and tech firms; LOD (formerly Lawyers on Demand) have taken a similar trajectory, both acquiring and divesting subsidiary ventures. Along with the US powerhouses Axiom and United Lex, LPO pathfinders Integreon and the fast-growing legal arms of the Big 4 accounting firms, these businesses are in the first rank of ALSPs. Together, they today present a significant and real competitive threat to established law firms, in terms of their ability to deliver the more commodity work but also in the dynamic and tech-enabled positioning they have forged through smart marketing and branding. On top of that potent threat, the Big 4 also weigh in with their vastly superior firm financial resources and established board and C-suite relationships right across the corporate world that are the envy of any individual law firm.

The impact of the emergence of credible, scale ALSPs on the advent of Agile law firms is two-fold. In order to combat the immediate and direct competitive threat to part of their business, law firms are having to respond by ditching many of their age-old assumptions about how they should resource, deliver and price many types of legal work. This is basically the defensive response reflex, but it is demonstrably changing law firms.

More proactively, law firms are reinventing their business model, or at least some parts of it, to emulate these alternative providers. We saw

"If the Agile law firm means anything it has to mean opening up the firm mindset and identifying, evaluating, trialling and launching new and different ways of delivering value to your clients."

this in the last decade when a rash of firms, especially in the United Kingdom, followed the early success of Lawyers on Demand, created by City firm Berwin Leighton Paisner, in creating their own flexible lawyering brands (Allen & Overy had Peerpoint, Eversheds had Agile, Pinsent Masons had Vario). More recently, a trend has emerged for firms to collect all of their various legal tech, legal operations consulting and alternative resourcing teams and ventures under newly formed and branded business units (Allen & Overy – again – have Fuse, TLT have FutureLaw, Osborne Clarke have OC Solutions). While there has been a whiff of window-dressing about some of these initiatives in the past, I think it is fair to say that the 2020 vintage realignment progressive firms are undertaking looks more radical, more likely to be permanent and more financially significant than previous moves. And, of course, more Agile – here we have large, successful established firms redesigning increasingly significant portions of their firm to work in ways that simply were not part of the law firm operating manual a few years ago. There is no hard-and-fast rule to how an Agile legal service firm should be structured or organised and a strong case for regularly reviewing and revising this to meet client demand and other external and internal stimuli.

This development was predicted and very impressively analysed in

"Amazon, Microsoft and Google are all in a strong position to create legal solution delivery businesses off the back of their existing dominant positions in the consumer and SME business markets."

Beaton and Kaschner's 2016 book *Remaking Law Firms: why and how*. The 'remade' law firm the authors anticipate in the title are defined as:

> *Remade law firms are those that have changed and diversified their business models, and in some respects are similar to NewLaw entities.*[79]

Just as the distinction we had got used to applying between law firms and ALSPs fades, so a new wave of alternatives to the time-honoured lawyer/law firm service is predicted to break. Sat on the periphery of the legal market, for now, is a collection of global giants who possess the financial heft, technology and innovation expertise and diversified business building track record to enter and disrupt just about any business sector. Their entry into the legal sector is no longer a matter of if, only of when. Amazon, Microsoft and Google are all in a strong position to create legal solution delivery businesses off the back of their existing dominant positions in the consumer and SME business markets. Major banks and insurers are also already offering legal services packaged into their services. Additionally, business tech providers like Intuit Quickbooks, Xero or Salesforce have pretty clear aspirations to offer an ever-extending range of smart, mobile, affordable and digital business services. Rounding off the line-up of the next wave of new competitors, LexisNexis and Thomson Reuters are two big public companies who already own vast quantities of legal data (far more than any single law firm) as well as an expanding range of technologies to point at that data. Their development of complex legal solutions that partially or entirely aim to cut lawyers and law firms out of the supply chain has been predicted for many years and will surely be one of the big trends of the next five years or so.

While we focus attention on the entertaining and diverting world of ALSPs and big legal services launches, investments and new entrants, we might run the risk of missing the most important competitive threat to private practice firms of the last – and no doubt the next – 10 years: the internal corporate legal department. With better resourced and led legal functions, a new generation of senior GC leaders in the corporate boardroom and the energising impact of embedded business professionals in 'legal operations' roles, today's corporate legal function is a very different beast. The steady encroachment, if that is not adopting the often grudging and adverse language law firms use, of corporate procurement functions into the legal service buying process has given this trend a push. Procurement departments have become more knowledgeable and capable in buying legal services and their relations with in-house legal departments less antagonistic over the years.

Alongside Agile law firms, we are seeing the emergence of Agile clients – flexing the way in which business issues with legal dimensions are handled using a mix of different in-house and external legal resources, technology and self-service tools. The era of corporate clients, indeed any clients, suffering under the inequality of the old legal seller/buyer relationship is almost over and assertive, data-rich and financially astute legal functions have emerged which have begun to redraw the contours of the legal marketplace, pulling work away from law firms who can't carry it out efficiently at the right price point. Much of that work has flowed in-house, as legal operations make the business for insourcing activity in order to release major savings. Corporate legal departments are now starting to select technology applications that enable them to efficiently deliver their legal services that would previously have had to go out to law firms. The selective use of ALSPs and contract attorney providers has provided an additional route to divert the pipeline of 'run the company' legal work that previously went to private practice firms. The presumption that the obvious route for legal work is going out to law firms has been questioned and then reversed. Today, for the most sophisticated corporations, turning to a law firm is now the final resort for the most specialised and least regular legal activity.

3. A new anatomy for your law firm – fit for the future

The theme of this section is about how to embrace the restless, radical, always-challenging spirit of Agile in your law firm. A continuous search for new and better ways of working and of delivering value to clients should be deep in the DNA of your organisation. One of the first steps is to search for those areas of your firm where you are relying on longstanding, unchallenged assumptions that this is the best way to work or, worse still, is simply 'the way we've always done it'. I am not suggesting you root out and turn upside down everything that is stable, established and works – your firm is a success today based on hard work and some strong foundations.

In some areas the forces of inertia tend to be strong and the will to improve and innovate weaker. I would highlight firm governance and management as one of these areas. Admittedly, some firms are constantly tweaking and changing – structure chart, department boundaries, job titles and geographic groupings seem to be in a constant state of flux. If you have worked in any of the Big 4 accounting/consulting firms (or, indeed, all of them – as I have) you will have been through the exhausting cycle of constant organisational changes. It is not a great recipe for stability and people can give up trying to understand this complex, constantly shifting place they work in. On the positive side, this fluidity is evidence of the restless search for better ways of working and of a willingness to adapt the most fundamental structures in response to changes in your environment.

"Strategic thinking and planning in an Agile firm become a whole-firm endeavour."

Law firms tend to sit at the 'steady as she goes' end of this spectrum, but all firms could take some time in the next six months to review how well their underlying business model serves the overriding mission of delivering value to clients – whether it encourages and actively drives autonomy, self-management and the Agile aim of making smart decisions as close to the client as you can; and whether it has adapted to reflect the changing world and the new skills and roles you need to achieve success in the 2020s.

Strategic thinking and planning in an Agile firm become a whole-firm endeavour. Released from being solely a senior leadership exercise, Agile strategy should be refocused on the client and insights and ideas sought from right across the business, most especially from those who work and maintain relationships with your clients. The trend for firm-wide innovation and ideation processes we have seen arrive in the legal sector, as well as for hackathons and design jam competitions, are good examples of the kind of activity that all firms could be doing as part of their strategy development and planning, as an alternative to the top-down financial spreadsheeting that is passed off as 'business planning' in too many firms.

I often refer to 'the new anatomy of the law firm' when I am consulting or speaking on this subject, but there is not one new default exoskeleton you should adopt. Instead, a constellation of options and models have evolved since the turn of the century that should be considered as you put your firm's structure under the microscope. In line with the Agile principles and the title of this section, take the blinkers off and be ready to be *restless*, *radical* and *challenging* in your search for a right model for your firm's future.

Entity model – in the UK market, almost nobody has been setting up a new law firm or legal services business as a partnership for the last five years. Partnerships, including LLPs, as a percentage of the total regulated firm population have been steadily shrinking and now stand at just over 50% of the total. The laws and regulations differ, of course, from country to country, but if your underlying business entity is something you have a choice over, then give some serious thought to the right model for the next decade. Do not just assume that you will always be a partnership. The reasons for firms incorporating are many and various – reduction in tax incentives, liability issues, desire to create some permanent capital value, ability to raise funds, merger, attractiveness to external investors, simplicity or wanting to make an emphatic statement that the firm is moving entirely away from the old 'partnership culture'.

At the heart of this question lies one of those 'business 101' questions that many law firms have had the luxury of not thinking about too deeply or too often – or have simply ignored as too difficult. That is the question of funding your firm. There is an undercurrent throughout this report that we are living, and managing, with very low levels of certainty, security and stability (the VUCA world). In that environment, a lot of previously unthinkable events now need to be thought about – 2020 made that very plain. Opportunities, too, are coming at us, with ever-narrowing 'windows', faster and with less warning. To manage any business, including a legal one, in this environment we cannot take financial results, retention of partners (and their capital) or benign banks for granted. Funding needs to be planned, with contingency and worst-case scenarios to cope with the Agile future we are facing. I have exhorted firms to begin this funding planning with the demand side of the equation – start with 'what will we need to invest in order to succeed, thrive, grow in the next 5+ years?'. Too often, discussions about funding start and end with supply side – 'what do we have/what will we get if these partners contribute more capital, or lose if these partners retire?'. Instead, you should work from your investment needs and then identify where that capital or cash will come from. This evaluation will then inform your thinking about equity, and perhaps entity, structure, especially if you identify a shortfall from internal sources for the funds you need to achieve your ambition. I should stress, though, that the funding/capital question is only one of the inputs to assessing the right entity for your firm going forward.

The periodic review and open, intelligent discussion of things as fundamental as the funding you need and the form of business entity you are, is a touchstone of how Agile your firm is. Your commitment to genuinely be the best you can be and adapt to changing circumstances, opportunities and choices is debatable if you still retain any 'sacred cows'. Even if you are not currently legally allowed to be anything other than a partnership, that may change within the next few years and thinking through your firm's stance is a sensible precaution and contingency. On top of that, many partnerships can already adopt more complex corporate-style group structures and holdings and that trend is taking off, as firms shift some parts of their practice into subsidiaries and spin-off companies that are better suited to that area of the firm than the 'one size fits all' partnership model. Examples range from legal department consulting arms to technology product spin-offs, from wholly-owned 'captive' business support centres to foreign subsidiaries which can take advantage of different regulatory frameworks.

4. Agile governance
There is no single prevailing governance model for law firm partnerships. There may not be a clear separation of executive and non-executive or oversight functions, although that is much more common today than it was at the turn of the century. Size of firm will, of course, dictate just how much complexity a firm needs or can handle. It will also tend to dictate whether the firm needs to deploy *representative governance*, where some owners/partners are elected to represent the interests of the whole shareholder body on a board. That said, even modestly sized firms have adopted this model, sometimes in order to restrict the distraction of firm management to just a small portion of their partners.

I have identified a trend towards a corporate governance approach in the last decade or so. Many firms have opted for a dual layer governance model starting with a small, core executive team, usually headed by and revolving around the senior executive (managing partner/chief executive). This team runs the firm day-to-day. Composition varies widely but the basic model is a senior executive plus his or her direct reports – typically heads of legal practice groups and business support functions. I have seen many where the lawyers are now in the minority, though I am an advocate of keeping a good balance here. Remember two important Agile principles. First, you are looking for a multi-disciplinary team with all the skill and experience you need to steer the firm in uncertain waters (to my mind that means that firms with almost all-lawyer executives and those with very few lawyers on them are both getting it wrong – though I appreciate how both models have evolved). Second, your firm is looking to maximise value to clients and key decisions and discussions should be constantly informed by the client perspective; so, make sure you have people informing your executive discussions who spend a lot of their time talking to, working with and serving clients. Hence my concern about firms which have begun to reduce the lawyer contingent on their executives to a minority.

Along with the composition of the executive team, its powers and name also vary widely. I have seen a move towards corporate terminology creeping into the legal sector and so we have a growing number of 'exco' (executive committee) and 'SLT' (senior leadership team) groups. 'Executive board' and 'central management team' are also popular. The right decision for your firm needs to suit your culture and style of language but do think hard about the old 'does what it says on the tin' adage. Does the label you use actually reflect not only what the role of the group is in the overall firm's mechanism but also your aspirations for its role and impact?

Over the next five years I expect law firm governance to go through another period of experimentation and evolution. Some of the following changes are already happening in parts of the profession, but will become more prominent and common, especially for those firms with an Agile mindset.

- Adoption of full corporate governance models, with the emphasis on strategic, risk and public ('licence to operate') oversight at board level. This effectively completes a switch from the board focusing primarily on shareholder/partner interests, to the board representing the interests of a much wider group of stakeholders. That echoes both the most recent trends in good corporate governance, as well as a strong movement within the legal sector for more socially aware and inclusive outcomes. Needless to say, this shift reflects some of the underlying principles of Agile organisations and their mission to reflect and respond to the world around them.
- Priority given to environmental, social and governance (ESG) objectives, reporting and investing standards, reflecting developments in the corporate world. The term ESG has been tied to climate change and resource scarcity, but it does cover much more including social issues, employment practices, diversity and inclusion, fraud, safety and data security, board diversity, executive pay and business ethics.
- Growth of independent non-executive board membership. A common trend in the last few years has been the appointment of non-executive directors (NEDs) to law firm boards or councils. In partnerships these roles are not legally directors and tend to play a slightly different, more advisory, role than in listed companies. In some cases, they are positioned as retained

advisers to either executive or board (NEDs can contribute very effectively at both levels in a law firm). The main impetus here is the recognition that a law firm's traditional leadership make-up lacks the breadth of experience, expertise and aptitude to steer increasingly large, complex, multi-national organisations. NEDs bring in new expertise to supplement the near-domination of lawyers/partners, most of whom have probably spent the majority of their career in the one firm and are often not diverse in terms of gender or ethnicity.

- Composition of the executive and oversight tiers will diverge. In many firms today I find the composition of an executive committee and a partnership board overlaps, sometimes up to 75% of the same faces sit on both. That undermines the operation of an effective oversight and governance process and suggests the firm really has not challenged the fundamental way it operates with any rigour. As more external, independent NEDs join boards and as the job of the executive morphs with the adoption of Agile principles, these two groups should become more distinct and more carefully composed to meet their specific aims.
- Rebalancing selection and election – at present, I still find most boards, and still quite a few executives, are elected in some way by partners. Even if those elections are, sometimes, a formality. Firms have begun to challenge the assumption that election is the right mechanism to create these fully functioning and multi-skilled teams that are so critical to the firm's future. Some powerful and successful executive leaders (managing partners/CEOs) have insisted on and won the right to select or appoint their direct reports and executive members, including practice group heads. In a parallel trend, senior partners or chairs are looking to ensure more balance and diversity of thought on boards by having at least some board roles into which they can appoint or nominate people from both inside and outside the firm, alongside the representatives who are still elected by their peers.
- Hiring external talent into the key leadership roles – there is a history of experimentation in the legal sector of hiring in external, sometimes 'non-lawyer' chief executives, managing partners and chairs. I am not going to try to unravel that history here. Suffice to say that not all of these experiments have ended well. Conversely, other senior leaders who came from outside are still in situ decades later, often having overseen some of the most dramatic law firm expansions. External hires into the top jobs are on the rise and I expect to see many more future law firm leaders, especially CEOs, hired in from other firms or from outside the profession. As firms in some countries float, take on private equity and shift their business model to become more

like tech companies or multi-disciplinary professional service firms, the need for leaders who are already experienced in these situations becomes greater. Some will be imposed by new external owners, some demanded by partners who know they need something different. Others will simply be the best candidate for the top job. The same logic applies to the board chair role too, which will begin to diverge from the elected senior partner model. Maybe some firms will look for executives and chairs with a track record in Agile transformation?

5. The next generation C-suite

Although you may not use the C-suite terminology of 'chief officers' in your firm and you may not refer to your senior business support managers collectively as the C-suite, you do still have one. In the 20 or so years since I took on the chief operating officer role at European law firm Osborne Clarke, the C-suite concept and many of the 'CxO' titles have become commonplace, not just among the largest global firms but spreading down to the mid-market. As the C-suite labels have become more ubiquitous in the corporate world and as firms have opened up their search criteria to welcome business professionals who have not previously served time in a law firm, so using the same terminology for these big jobs makes more sense.

"An increasing number of firms have switched the managing partner title to CEO or chief executive."

An increasing number of firms have switched the managing partner title to CEO or chief executive. Some have used the change to highlight a clear change in the remit of the senior executive role. In other cases, the renaming symbolises a wider transition to a more business-like structure. Those symbolic changes make sense and can really help mark a break with the past. But a well-defined senior law firm executive role can just as effectively be labelled 'managing partner'. And some clients and contacts can get a little confused about whether the CEO of their law firm has the standing of a partner (of course, most law firm CEOs are partners).

Other C-suite titles have followed. Chief financial officer (CFO) and chief information officer (CIO) are now regularly used, either simply as rebadged alternatives to finance director and IT director respectively, or to signify, as with the CEO change, some more fundamental rethinking of the role. Larger firms may have a CFO and a finance director, a CIO and an IT director, with the C-suite role taking on the more strategic, often international remit. Outside the United States, I have found firms a little slower to adopt chief people officer and chief marketing officer titles and I sense that is down to both some uncertainty about what these roles should include and a lingering perception, misplaced in my view, among lawyers that these senior HR and marketing roles don't justify the same level of executive status as finance or technology. As a result, most firms seem to have a patchwork of different senior executive titles – often having a managing partner, CFO and CIO, HR director, head of marketing all on the same org chart. I am not convinced how many firms have taken a few steps back to reconsider all the ways in which they could make their executive structures simpler, clearer, easier to navigate and understand – and more effective in creating an Agile environment.

The chief operating officer (COO) role, where my own main executive experience sits pre-consulting days, arrived in law firms in the 1990s and 2000s. COOs are focused on coordination and collaboration of a whole series of disparate business functions and on aligning and streamlining support to the lawyers and, indirectly, to clients. Efficiency and cost management are high on the COO's priority list too – smart procurement, use of outsourcing or captive shared service centres, minimising duplication and over-capacity and trying to shift partnerships off their 'just buy whatever the partners and clients ask for' mindset.

Today, most large firms have some type of COO in position, though the scope of legal COO portfolios vary widely. At its most extensive, the law firm COO remit effectively takes on a large portion of the responsibilities of the hands-on managing partner, allowing the latter to focus on growth, hiring, strategy execution and client/legal practice development, while the COO 'runs the shop', from finance through technology and buildings, people, risk and business development. Although some legal COOs have the 'full-fat' scope outlined here, plenty of others have a cut-down role profile, with finance and marketing/business development commonly sitting with a parallel C-suite colleague.

A word about COOs and Agile. Generally, I'd advocate that firms who find intensifying pressure on their managing partner and other partners in executive roles, seriously consider reducing that stress point by hiring or promoting into a COO role, scaling back the management time spent by partners, including the managing partner, and getting them refocused back towards clients, the delivery of Agile legal services and strategy execution. From an Agile perspective this achieves multiple factors:

- Gets your scarce management and leadership skills refocused back where you need them – on the client and the innovating and transforming of how your firm delivers service and value to them.
- Takes often over-stretched and often simply underskilled lawyers out of operational management duties that they are not trained for or happy doing.
- Creates a role which is focused on coordination, collaboration, alignment of your disparate business functions – often previously run as silos competing for the managing partner's attention and favour.
- Catalyses the transition of your executive team into an Agile multi-disciplinary team, with the addition of the COO's business management skillset, especially if you are hiring in talent from another sector or type of firm, and a clear emphasis on operating as a seamless, aligned team.
- Provides the opportunity to reassess all the functions, internal services and processes in the firm as you develop the COO's scope and remit. This is the time to re-evaluate what decisions and activities can be decentralised, closer to the client and client-facing legal teams, and what *should* be centralised to create more client-focused time and bandwidth in those same teams.

One of the most fascinating trends of recent years for those of us who study law firm organisation and governance is just how many new C-suite and senior management roles have popped up, in the wake of the legal COO. Your firm may not feel large enough or wealthy enough to go out into the job market and hire someone into these very focused, highly specialised executive positions. They have been the preserve of the larger national and international firms so far.

For the smaller firm, the following list of emerging new law firm executive roles may seem a bit fantastical. Hand-on-heart, these *are* all existing roles in law firms. Numbers with each title are increasing and I predict they will continue to do so. In the largest firms these roles can be C-suite 'chief officers', underlining the high value firms place on these jobs and the competitive job market for them – firms have needed to deliver up prestige job titles and remuneration packages to get in the talent they want. In other firms these jobs are second tier management, reporting into the C-suite for now.

I absolutely acknowledge that many firms will not be in a position to dedicate someone to these roles, still less go out into the market and hire in an experienced specialist. But there is another way to read and think about this section and every reader can do this – work out who in your firm has responsibility for this remit and follow up with them. In all cases, these areas of business performance are already very important and becoming more so. So, there is no opt-out, no 'this probably isn't very important for us'. You may not have the scale to justify a chief information security officer or chief client experience officer but who holds this responsibility within their overall remit? Ideally, I would ask every firm to amend their role profiles so that they clearly state "*incorporating* chief X officer responsibilities, as follows".

Chief digital officer (CDO)/chief technical officer (CTO) – although the CIO (information) designation is the most popular, and still growing, designation for senior technology professionals in law firms, some firms have started to revisit the tech roles. Firms with a focus on broad digital transformation, and especially on delivering that transformation as part of their client service, might opt for chief digital officer as the right label for the most senior technology executive. Firms with chief digital or technology officers include Freshfields, Linklaters, KPMG, Accenture, Pinsent Masons, Ashurst,

Chief information security officer/chief data officer – one of the biggest recent trends is the overdue acknowledgement of information and cyber security as an existential challenge to businesses across so many sectors. Legal, long regarded as an easy target for corporate espionage and hacking, is a prime example and we are finally seeing security raised to the status of a regular board and executive agenda item. The link between deploying top-quality information security skills and Agile is direct, with every step forward in information transparency, insight-generation and data enablement of both clients and client-facing teams your firm needs to take at least an equal step up in security. The rise of the chief data officer (yet another CDO!) recognises not just the need to protect data but also the concomitant opportunity to exploit and leverage it. Again, it represents a recognition that leading this effort in a professional firm is becoming too big a job to simply fall to a generic IT management team. Firms with chief information security or chief data officers include Allen & Overy, Slaughter & May, Deloitte, Norton Rose Fulbright, Pinsent Masons, PwC, Stephenson Harwood.

Chief innovation officer (CINO)/chief transformation officer – multiple senior titles have been spawned by law firms over the last three to five years as innovation has become such a commonly cited business objective. These roles are at the heart of the Agile transformation. Firms have tried encompassing firmwide innovation leadership within an expanded scope for IT, operations or knowledge and in some cases those reconfigured responsibilities are working. A consensus has formed, though, that a genuine innovation or transformation effort needs strong, independent leadership that is not confined within any of what are perceived as 'legacy' functional silos. Indeed, I have encountered a lot of bruised egos and fallout from personality clashes over the rights to 'innovation' leadership in the last few years. Creating a top-level executive role responsible for innovation delivers a strong message to everyone in your firm, as well as to your clients. It also raises expectations and runs the risk that big plans and promises are made before the hard yards of researching, listening, developing hypotheses and iterating and delivering change has begun. That is not the Agile way and I suspect too many big innovation initiatives have fallen foul of this trap. Perhaps the most important lesson learned so far is that one individual is unlikely ever to be the answer – they can have a significant impact but top-down support and change to many other aspects of the firm, as this report has explored, is a necessary precondition to success in innovation. Firms with CINOs include Blank Rome, Simpson Thacher Bartlett, Macfarlanes, Family Law Partners (UK), Freshfields, Kennedys IQ, Bryan Cave Leighton Paisner, Faegre Drinker, Dentons.

Chief client service/experience/excellence officer – aligned and sometimes occupying some of the same territory as the innovation portfolio, these roles are beginning to appear in law firm org charts. They follow a route mapped by the Agile champion and customer-obsessed tech giants, in hard-wiring the customer perspective into their organisation design. Rather than simply exhorting a client-focused mindset, these appointments give someone real power inside the business to be the client champion. I like these moves, which seem to me to plug a long-standing gap in the law firm ecosystem – who in leadership really takes the client's part – practice heads, managing partner, marketing/business development are all conflicted in some ways (not least having an intense performance focus on getting more work and fees from those clients). The 'client success officer' variant is interesting, and again echoes tech and other new economy sectors – this role focuses on how the firm maximises the client's business

"Multiple senior titles have been spawned by law firms over the last three to five years as innovation has become such a commonly cited business objective."

success by bringing all the firm's services, expertise and value-add to bear. That is a key component of the Agile mission and firms who find it tough to get that client-centric, Agile mindset really embedded should consider whether they need to make a senior, perhaps partner-level, appointment to drive it. Firms with chief client officers include Baker McKenzie, Wiggin, Miller Nash Graham and Dunn, Baker Donelson, Dentons, Baker Botts, Steptoe & Johnson, Norton Rose Fulbright, Troutman Pepper, McCarthy Tetrault, Eversheds.

Chief pricing officer – the advent of intense price pressure from GCs and the emergence of alternative fee arrangements, amplified by the global financial crisis, meant that many firms found themselves in uncharted territory. Having spent a career billing by the clock, some of them found clients demanding, or imposing, fixed or capped fees. Some massive losses followed as people with no real planning or estimating capability took big hits due to poor quoting and poor matter management. Things have improved, a bit, as firms have geared up to use data analytics and disciplines like legal project management (LPM). Both clients and firms have handed over much of the data-crunching, information exchange and even negotiation to specialist functions – legal operations in corporate legal and pricing/LPM in law firms. A host of large US and global firms – too many to mention – have appointed chief pricing officers to steer these teams and help improve pricing methods, education and practice. A closely related development is the appointment of a chief analytics officer or chief practice management officer, working on the information/insight/impact model I explored earlier. In a world where data just may be 'the new oil', putting top-tier analytics capability high on your firm's shopping list makes sense. Firms with chief pricing officers or chief analytics officers include White & Case, Covington & Burling, Mayer Brown, Greenberg Traurig, Freshfields, Withers, Womble Bond Dickinson, Bryan Cave Leighton Paisner, Perkins Coie.

Chief diversity officer – the profession has taken its own sweet time to make meaningful moves on all kinds of diversity. As I noted before, progress in gender equality at entry level has not been reflected higher up the ladder and the ethnic and social make-up of law firms are some way from reflecting the societies they serve. Firms had begun to take this issue more seriously before 2019 but the successive game-changing impacts of Me Too/Time's Up, Black Lives Matter and the social dislocation that followed the outbreak of COVID-19 have seen it rocket up the leadership's agenda. As with many other 'tough nut to crack' issues where you need to shift an entire organisation's mindset, the appointment of a dedicated officer for diversity and inclusion may become necessary to help you break through, rather than asking HR to try to solve this challenge. Increasing diversity of thought, experience and perspective is critical to creating an Agile organisation and firms will need to address the obstacle presented by their current shortcomings on the journey to agility. Firms with chief diversity officers or similar include Sidley Austin, Reed Smith, Shearman & Sterling, Winston & Strawn, Bryan Cave Leighton Paisner, Shoosmiths, DLA Piper.

General counsel/chief risk officer – it has been interesting to see larger law firms adapt the legal and regulatory structures of some of their large clients. More firms now have their senior legal risk role structured similarly to a corporate GC or chief risk officer. Firms with GCs/chief risk officers include Osborne Clarke, Walkers, Irwin Mitchell, Dentons, Bates Wells.

Legal project management/legal operations – although less often badged as a C-suite role, law firms have been expanding their LPM functions and creating more senior and influential executive roles leading the line. In some firms, LPM slots in under the chief pricing or practice management officer role and adds significantly to the team that role has responsibility for. In other firms the global or national head of LPM role has become a substantial management post. 'Legal operations' is a term usually associated with the operations and finance roles within corporate legal departments. But in the last few years law firms have begun to co-opt the terminology to reflect their largest client's organisations and we have seen legal operations used to designate client-facing LPM functions or law firm-based consultants who assist clients develop their own in-house operations. Firms with senior LPM/legal operations roles include Norton Rose Fulbright, Ashurst, Addleshaw Goddard, Mayer Brown, DLA Piper, Dentons, Hogan Lovells and Allen & Overy.

Legal engineer/legal solutions architect – two of the fastest growing legal industry designations are this pair of job titles. That highlights the traction that Agile principles have already had across the legal sector. Legal engineers are being hired, redeployed from lawyer, paralegal and tech roles and trained up through apprenticeship and intern programmes on an increasing scale. They are working with Agile, Lean, Design thinking, Lean Start-Up, LPM and Six Sigma methodologies and an ever-widening set of applications, including those with AI and machine learning built-in. These roles span geographies, though with particular growth in the United States and United Kingdom. And they are being utilised across a spectrum of firms, from the largest Big Law players to high-volume insurance and conveyancing outfits. Not long ago, these roles felt like they exclusively belonged to alternative legal service providers (ALSPs) and legal techs, but are now being adopted at a fast pace by law firms. That is evidence of the changed world we are living in – anything that works for ALSPs in driving forward innovation, agility and response to market needs is being picked up rapidly by law firms. Law firms are internalising, developing and often industrialising those ideas and innovations. To some extent this fast-growing corps of engineers, architects and solution providers are the vanguard of the Agile revolution.

At this early stage, these legal engineer roles are not confined by precedent and individual job descriptions, and the routes to them vary a lot. The United Kingdom tends to prefer 'engineer' and the United States 'solutions architect', but the jobs are similar. As the role sits at the interface between law and technology, it is not surprising that legal engineering teams mix people with backgrounds in law (whether as a qualified attorney or as a paralegal or legal graduate) and in tech. There tends to be a preference for legal engineers to have a background in law, but the firms who are hiring and developing engineers stress they are ready to develop the parts of the legal/tech overlap that joiners don't yet have. I am impressed by the rapidly growing number of degree students and young lawyers who are well aware of and interested in these roles – there is a 'third track' legal career path forming, a new hybrid of legal and technology competencies, which will transform our definition of lawyer over the next five to 10 years. It would not be surprising, by the end of this decade, to find that "we are all legal engineers now!"

Agile first steps – restless, radical and challenging
- Set up a review of the best entity, funding, organisational structure model for your firm over the next decade. Do not put this off (the decade will be over!) or assume the answer is obvious. Apply Agile principles of open-minded, radical thinking before identifying a set of potential options, however uncomfortable or unlikely they initially sound. Schedule the next review for a few years' time – this is no longer a 'once in a generation' decision.
- Lead from the front – are you and the senior team at your firm being seen as 'restless, radical and challenging' and pushing towards an Agile future? Take some first steps – there are a lot of areas of organisational design and operations listed in this chapter that might be well overdue rethinking. Get started.
- Invest some time into a strategic review of what the alternative legal service providers are doing and the products emerging from them, legal techs and other law firms: what can your firm learn and adopt yourselves? Which of these new products and services are directly in your markets and what impact will they have?
- Review your org chart and line-up of key roles and responsibilities against the roll-call of emerging 21st-century roles covered in this chapter. Who is covering these remits and where are your gaps? Be prepared to plan a steady programme of restructuring as these areas of firm management become more fundamental.

X. Digital

1. Digital transformation

The final two Agile Attribute chapters are relatively short. That is not because these are less important topics. Far from it – both the smart deployment of technology in modern legal services and aligning your firm around a guiding and overriding purpose are nothing short of imperatives. They are, however, imperative for *every* law firm to get right, regardless of whether you are embarking on an Agile journey or not. In discussions about this report, colleagues wondered whether these were even strictly speaking Agile Attributes for that reason. Ultimately, though, I decided firmly to include them in my 10-point prescription because they are essential preconditions to successful agility.

In the case of technology, this report is not about IT or the need to digitalise. But, as you will have read in the chapters above, the impact of technology and its role in enabling Agile change is indispensable. Digitisation is critical. Clients expect it, and those expectations have boomed in the period since COVID-19 lockdown placed so many of our populations in their homes, reliant on computers, mobile devices and apps to connect with the outside world and maintain a semblance of normal life. Law firms I work with have noted that waves of previously digitally-reluctant clients, many of them elders (but also the most personable and extrovert captains of industry), have now entered the digital age. We are emerging into an era where demand for slick and accessible digital services is going to be nearly ubiquitous.

Your people also expect a seamless and connected digital experience throughout the organisation. In a 2021 Williams Lea/Sandpiper survey of over 400 people, 79% believed that the COVID-19 period had led to greater acceptance of new processes, technology and ways to work.[80] The reliance on remote working to keep businesses running has stimulated improvements in the functionality of the tech, but also dramatic leaps in the tech capabilities of the workforce. As with your client-base, the biggest change is among the group previously most reluctant to truly engage with IT. That does not mean we magically now have an entire working population who think and act like digital natives, but it has wiped out any residual concern about rolling out digital tools and solutions on the basis that some of your partners and lawyers would not cope. Now, you can be fairly sure that they will cope – somehow – and if they don't, their careers as successful lawyers in the 2020s look likely to be short-lived. These are the conditions required to achieve a breakthrough *digital transformation* in your firm.

In *Successful Digital Transformation in Law Firms: A Question of Culture*,[81] legal innovation leader Isabel Parker lays out not only the case for urgent digital transformation but also practical advice on how

"As digital transformation washes over every sector, so Agile cultures, structures and models will follow."

to effect meaningful and sustainable change. Her view of the post-COVID-19 world is that:

> *the crisis has reinforced the importance of agility and resilience, and the critical role digital technologies play in client service. For law firms, digital transformation should no longer be viewed as an indulgence, but as an urgent necessity.*

Agility has gone hand-in-hand with digitisation in most places and more tech businesses have, unsurprisingly, embraced Agile principles than probably any other sector. As digital transformation washes over every sector, so Agile cultures, structures and models will follow.

So, technology is important. But too many firms are rushing to buy or develop tech, assuming it will deliver results and success. It never will be a panacea. Winners and losers in most sectors, including law, are not generally distinguished by their level of access to either technology or data. Applying technology to a bad process and without discovering the client's needs is not going to help. The Agile message has a kernel of patience in it. Get started now, absolutely, but don't expect that you can short-cut to success. If you don't put in the hard yards of using empathy, listening and discovery to understand the real experiences and problems your clients have, no amount of AI and smart tech tools are going to help you do the right things. I have a concern that too many law firms are tempted to take that short-cut route and find the emphasis on taking the time to design, innovate and improve based on deep learning and listening too difficult and challenging. It was good to hear a law firm director of IT, Sarah Blair of Thorntons Law, underline that "the way to deliver value is to really understand the unmet and unsaid needs of our clients. To do that you need a deep, human-centred approach".[82]

At the same virtual event in 2020 Christina Blacklaws, former President of The Law Society of England and Wales and now a strategy consultant, quoted the Twilio digital engagement survey that concluded:

> *COVID-19 was the digital accelerant of the decade. COVID-19 accelerated companies' digital communications strategy by an average of 6 years while 97% of enterprise decision makers believe the pandemic sped up their company's digital transformation.*[83]

Leading legal IT consultant Peter Owen also cited a recent survey statistic that suggested just 15% of the workforce could be permanently office-based going forward.[84]

There are multiple ways in which this dramatic digital transformation has affected the legal sector since the onset of COVID-19, including:

- onboarding clients digitally and entirely online;
- digital courts and virtual hearings;
- increased take-up and demand for cloud computing;
- replacement of fixed and desktop IT equipment with laptops and mobile devices;
- Agile working;
- video meetings;
- connected communications with our distributed people and with clients; and
- more intensive use of encryption and information security tools.

2. The impact of technology on legal work

We hear a lot these days about the various predictions of just how far AI and other technologies will be able to replace lawyers and other humans in the legal workflow. The debate will continue for years to come, while all the time the utilisation of digital labour and human labour is shifting beneath our feet, in the favour of the former. There is a lot of talk about 'lawyer substitutes', referencing either robot lawyers or new alternative legal services that replicate all the functions and services of the traditional law firm. But that is not the prevailing pattern of substitution. Rather it is *partial* substitution that is affecting us most rapidly and, by its very nature, more imperceptibly. This trend is most pronounced in the highly specialised legal markets, initially targeting the more routine, volume and commoditised legal tasks. Here services are being delivered faster, cheaper and better than they have been to-date by dialling-up the mix of technology. That shift to more tech-led delivery has spawned new markets in discovery and document review, online document provision, contract management and analytics and employment law advisory.

The impact of partial substitution leading to permanent erosion of the body of work lawyers do is mirrored by the latest thinking about how technology, across a much broader landscape, is replacing the working activity of human beings. Daniel Susskind takes this question as one of the central themes of his 2020 book, *A World Without Work*.[85] He explains the latest, revelatory economic and scientific thinking about the impact of AI and focuses on the transformative implications of partial, incremental substitution of human labour by technology. AI engineers and academics have shifted away, in recent years, from the primary focus that had dominated the early years of AI and obsessed mankind – can we build machines that replicate the human brain and think like us? That obsessive quest led to some great discoveries but also long periods of relative inertia (such as the 'AI Winter' of the late 20th century). The prevailing hypothesis said that machines would only be able to undertake human activity that was routine – as a result jobs were often categorised into those that were relatively routine – more likely to be displaced – and those that were not.

"Developing a machine to successfully achieve one very particular task at or above human level is now the direction of travel."

AI thinking, research and commercial product development is now concentrated not on the elusive search for a human-like *General AI*, but on the development of specific, niche but successful *Narrow AI* instances. These may take on and beat human capability in limited, specific and, at first glance, ancillary activity. But they are doing so now at great speed – from the landmark attention-grabbing AI success at beating human champions in complex games like Chess, Go and Jeopardy to the series of breakthroughs that are now enabling driverless cars and drone deliveries. Developing a machine to successfully achieve one very particular task at or above human level is now the direction of travel. If a human activity, or job, involves 20 such tasks then the automation route will be to develop 20 'machines', not try to develop one all-singing, all-dancing machine that can do all 20 of those things. Human activity is broken-down and can then be undertaken by many different machines or programmes. The development cycle of these machines is getting faster all the time, opening up the prospect of all 20 tasks – the whole job – being performed better by machines in a shorter timeframe than we had imagined possible until recently. These breakthroughs in computer design tactics are likely to erode the work of many jobs, including lawyers, faster but perhaps more subtly than we had expected.

There are some obvious Agile consequences of these trends in the emergence of new technology and new business models that can substitute a lawyer. One is that both clients and their legal service providers have a myriad of new options and combinations of sources and resources. As credible alternative legal service providers (ALSPs) have developed, the range of options a corporate client can choose from to deliver their legal needs has expanded. Many of these ALSPs have a much higher proportion of technology in their delivery mix, compared to the prevailing law firm model which places more reliance on human resources. The next step, which I expect will dominate the direction of legal provision in the 2020s, is for all legal service delivery to be performed by smart new *combinations* of technology and humans. Practices and teams within law firms need to analyse and refine their optimum human labour/digital labour mix and keep doing so constantly going forward.

This is not dystopian or alarmist. We are at a point where legal and business technologies have already embedded themselves deep enough into even the smaller law office to mean that every law firm is now processing mainly digital inputs using a combination of people and technology and delivering advice and documents as primarily digital outputs. The shift to remote working in 2020 reinforced and cemented the dominance of entirely digital inputs, processes and outputs in modern legal work. Contrary to what some lawyers still claim, there is no 'human only' legacy option to defend or promote as being better; the entire profession has already shifted to what we could describe as a cyborg, bionic or digitally enhanced service.

The ability of applications to automate and replace some lawyer tasks and activities has already resulted in the digital labour component of some legal services, say high volume litigation or contract management, being 50% or higher. Technology is still augmenting, rather than entirely replacing the lawyer, but there are almost endless choices of points on the spectrum of human/digital labour mix for firms and their clients to select from. As competition shifts, pricing pressure increases and new and enhanced technologies continue to flood onto the market (often becoming more affordable and commoditised at the same time), law firms need to regularly re-evaluate the best mix and implement changes – changes that will impact on organisation, resourcing, hiring, process, pricing and more – not just on IT. Law firms have to take an extremely Agile stance on this most fundamental of decisions – the digital/human labour mix – and consign the idea of fixed legal team resourcing to the bin.

We are likely to see the numbers of junior lawyers hired into firms to start falling, something that has already begun at entry level and the dislocating impact of COVID-19 has complicated, especially as more people switch to Agile, remote and location-agnostic working patterns. Some clients have pushed back at paying for the work that inexperienced lawyers do and firms can't rely on the pyramid structure and leverage in the same way they once did – something that is causing economic stress inside many firms as it becomes harder to generate the multiples partners could expect historically. There is a strong parallel in the steadily falling profit margins that the otherwise hugely successful Big 4 accounting firms have been seeing over the last decade. The broad associate base of the law firm pyramid has traditionally been leveraged to the point that it was the primary revenue and profit generating demographic. This dependence on a large body of human resources underpinning the law firm model is giving way to something else, but there are no truly proven alternative models.

Firms will need to employ Agile principles to experiment with, iterate and improve on these alternatives. What Jordan Furlong calls with his tongue only slightly in his cheek, "the post-lawyer law firm" is approaching.[86] Maybe it is at the extreme end of the spectrum, but the assumption and convention that law firms are quintessentially collections of lawyers is now being challenged in multiple ways. The legal market does not exist to provide work for lawyers – a law firm run entirely for its lawyers is a case of supply in search of demand.

"The shift to remote working in 2020 reinforced and cemented the dominance of entirely digital inputs, processes and outputs in modern legal work."

One of the most frequent analogies I use in my presentations to legal conferences starts with a hypothetical newlaw start-up. This new firm has a great, innovative business proposition, a smart and experienced lawyer/entrepreneur founder team and some investor cash behind them. They are about to make their first senior hire, post start-up, and have a choice of where to place this limited investment. They could hire an experienced fee-earning senior lawyer from a big firm, or a technology star with experience of setting up business tech that connects service providers and clients, or a digital marketing specialist with a proven track record of building a professional service brand online. Nine times out of 10, the lawyer will be the last pick because that role can be filled by any number of people out there in the existing legal market – located, hired and plugged into the structure. The other two skillsets are rarer and, frankly, more essential to this new firm's success as a new entrant into the ultra-competitive market of the 2020s. This marks the next step in the inexorable 'death of difference', where law firms are becoming less distinct, unique and insulated from the way the wider business world works.

In these models the individual lawyer is to some extent a 'plug and play' component. While that is a hallmark of many of the growing newlaw models it is also, let's be honest, already true in most of today's large highly corporatised law firms too. That's not to suggest that big, market leading law firms don't still rely on the high wattage star power of name partners, but that they have expanded to a scale and structure now where the firm's brand, process and infrastructure is playing as big a part in their success as the individual stars. The Big 4 accounting firms have, of course, taken this road many years ago.

If we apply the Agile mindset and think about the law firm as whatever vehicle works most effectively to solve the legal problems and meet the needs that clients have, it can take a whole variety of shapes and structures. There is no reason to shackle this delivery of great legal solutions by limiting yourselves to the constraints set by the conventional law firm model, including the need for ranks of lawyers as the dominant resource pool. It is no longer left-field or futuristic for your leadership to ask and address fundamental questions like 'how do we make money while we sleep?', 'how can we monetise our data assets?', 'what does productisation of our legal services look like?', or 'can we deliver greater value to our clients and our owners with fewer lawyers and more technology?' Law firms can now draw on consolidated banks of knowledge, technology and data analytics to bring to bear on client deliverables. Not all service delivery requires lawyer resources. The question for today and tomorrow is whether your law firm knows which services are which and is planning for its future based on the optimum mix of these components.

Agile first steps – digital
- Plan how you will finalise the complete digitisation of your processes, ensuring that all work can be completed and delivered digitally, even if paper will sometimes be used as a valuable additional media.
- Engage all of your IT, innovation and legal tech teams completely in your Agile journey, ensuring there is comprehensive training on and engagement with the Agile toolkit included in this report.
- Initiate a strategic review, incorporating IT, HR and legal teams, of the evolution of your firm's digital/human labour mix over the next decade. Take control of this issue, while remaining Agile and responsive to social and technological change.

XI. United by a common purpose

1. Aligning with purpose
For successful Agile organisations the purpose shared by all in this 10th and final Agile Attribute takes us right back to the first Attribute – being client-centric. It is natural, and probably most powerful, if the 'northstar' that unites all parts of the firm embodies a genuine passion for serving clients.

This purpose has to be embedded and embraced across the entire organisation in order to support the achievement of organisational agility. That means that individuals throughout the firm – not just partners or lawyers – can each identify what that aim means for them and their team and proactively take action to progress towards it. Your purpose connects everyone with each other and with your clients.

All successful organisations, Agile or not, should be founded on a common, unifying purpose. Some strategists refer to this as mission and vision, others as your 'winning ambition' or even a BHAG (big hairy audacious goal). But purpose is not exactly the same. It goes further. It answers the all-important question: *why do we exist?* Many people assume, wrongly, that a company or firm exists to make money. While this is an important result of a firm's existence, you have to go deeper and find the real reasons for your being to arrive at purpose.

Values

Multiple studies in the last five years or so have demonstrated that 'purpose-driven companies' have higher market share and grow faster than competitors. They also score consistently higher on employee and client customer satisfaction. One of the best-known business quotes of the century so far comes from Simon Sinek, the influential creator of *Start with Why* and one of the most-watched TED talks ever. It sits at the centre of my work and approach to advising clients. Without understanding and internalising it I think it will be very difficult to make the Agile journey: "People don't buy what you do; they buy *why you do it* and what you do simply *proves* what you believe."[87]

I would heartily recommend a dive into *Start with Why*[88] and Sinek's other works. The result should be a purpose that is clear, differentiated from other organisations (especially your competitors), authentic and inspiring. Too often I encounter a purpose, or mission statement, that is too vague and anodyne – impossible to connect specifically to that firm. Lots of businesses end up trying to cover all the bases, appeal to all constituencies and craft a sequence of great-sounding words. The result is usually generic. Law firms have a particular habit of believing they have perfectly captured their distinctive and attractive culture, only for their statement to sound exactly like every other law firm.

The purpose of an Agile firm should not be generic or anodyne. This isn't a strap-line for your corporate brochure or to tick the box of some hired-in strategy consultant (including me). Your purpose is going to need to work hard. It is there to integrate all the multiple, moving parts of your firm. In an Agile setting, purpose will align your loose, connected network of teams. It will keep them all focused on the same issues and give them some defined guiderails and direction of travel. For you to liberate your teams, emphasising their self-management and autonomy, you need to provide the stability and certainty of a single, universal and inspiring purpose for all. That is why getting this right is even more critical for the Agile firm.

You may have done a lot of thinking and surfaced your firm's purpose a long time ago. You may be undertaking that effort now, perhaps triggered by the disruption you have experienced in the last year or so. At firms that are yet to start down the Agile road, lacking a clearly stated purpose and direction can be a severe limitation. You need to agree and articulate that purpose and it needs to closely align with the Agile future you are visualising and aiming at.

2. Purpose into practice – being Agile about becoming Agile
John Hagel, consultant and Director of Deloitte's Center for the Edge, has spent years writing about the application of Agile principles in practice and how larger organisations specifically can protect

> *"'Purpose-driven companies' have higher market share and grow faster than competitors."*

themselves against the natural 'tissue rejection' of transformative new ways of working. His studies of these transformation efforts reveal the high failure rate of 'top down, big bang' approaches. He tags the alternative approach he proposes "scaling the edge".[89] That means focusing on first transforming at the edges of the organisation, rapidly and radically, and uses the pull of success at the edges to gradually engage more and more of the core; ultimately, the edge has scaled to the point where it has become the new core.

In his book *The Age of Agile* Steven Denning notes that surveys carried out by the SD Learning Consortium show that 80 to 90% of Agile teams currently perceive tension between the way the Agile teams function and the way the whole organisation operates.[90] Unless the tension is resolved, it can lead to abrupt abandonment of an organisational commitment to Agile altogether. As Clayton Christensen famously explained in his seminal text *The Innovator's Dilemma*, it is notoriously difficult for established, previously very successful market leaders to pivot to a new model and market effectively.[91]

What do these lessons learned from the growth of Agile in other organisations mean for you? You will need the top of your firm fully engaged and supportive of any major transformation effort. That much, I know, already sounds obvious. What has been proven time and again not to work, however, is what John Hagel refers to as the "top down, big bang" approach.[92] Huge firm-wide transformation initiatives, without the build-up of demand and enthusiasm from team-level, have a tendency to crash and burn. Aiming to become an Agile organisation with a loose network of self-managed highly empowered teams cannot, logically, originate in a huge, imposed programme delivered from the top.

As I arrive at the end of this report, I hardly need to make another plea for firms to apply Agile principles and thinking. This short segment provides a few ideas specifically about using Agile techniques as you implement an Agile approach across your firm. It is a classic example of 'walking the talk' and ensuring that your colleagues and clients will not be able to point at you or any of your leadership team and justifiably accuse you of saying one thing and actually doing another.

Get the leadership fully on board – as with every aspect of becoming an Agile organisation I have covered earlier in this report, implementation requires leadership to be squarely behind the programme and adopting not just the Agile mindset, but Agile behaviours and tools in advance of the rest of the firm. Adopting

"Change a small number of things at a time. Test, gather feedback and iterate the design."

Agile working practices such as sprints and daily stand-ups, orientating the firm definitively towards client needs and expectations and offering early examples of greater empowerment and engagement are all things firm leaders are well able to do promptly.

Start small, test and iterate – as with any Agile process, implementing Agile teams in your firm should resemble a fast, discrete experiment. Change a small number of things at a time. Test, gather feedback and iterate the design. You are proving the concept and demonstrating how Agile works. Running a pilot in a particularly suitable or enthusiastic team, practice area or region makes a lot more sense than attempting a big bang, which risks breaking most of the Agile rules. This approach also allows you to develop skilled champions, coaches and advocates who can help other areas of the firm get on board.

Listen to and act on feedback – whether you are running your initial pilot internally without direct engagement with the client or taking a bolder route and partnering with clients, you will need to build feedback channels and the Build-Measure-Learn loop into your roll-out. Your internal audience in particular will be watching carefully how you deal with negative feedback and the identification of blockages and problems. Needless to say, these should be handled using Agile principles – taken seriously, added to the backlog, prioritised and solved, ideally by your multi-disciplinary Agile team themselves.

Selecting the team – give yourselves the best possible chance of success in the early days by carefully selecting Agile teams that have the experience, attitude and blend of skills and personality to deliver a real improvement on the old ways of working. Am I suggesting 'packing the team' somehow with super-stars? Not quite – the Agile team in, say, consumer real estate should not be made up of some Agile mercenary group parachuted in from all the other parts of your firm and beyond. But do give your local team the best possible support and ensure they have the full range of competences required for their project, pulling in specialists from around the firm and ensuring that they have an Agile coach with experience. Ensure training and education prior to starting is adequate and the tools, digital and otherwise (maybe including a space and facilities to run a Kanban board), are available. Ensure training is followed up very quickly by real hands-on practical experience – Agile skills need to be used and seen in action.

3. What now?

Why does agility still represent such a big and daunting challenge for law firms? There are some good reasons, which I mentioned right at the start of this report, why the law firm model provides a decent starting point for transitioning to an Agile organisation, compared to many corporations. A network of the small team framework is in place and there is already a strong commitment to being client-centred. Practitioners spend a lot of time with their clients in most areas of practice and have plentiful opportunities to get to know them, often seeing them at their best and at their worst – 'warts and all'. There is a public service ethos running through the profession that still flourishes in most firms, though it does have to bend or give way to the dominant pursuit of partner profit more often than most law firms like to admit.

But the obstacles to agility are tough to overcome, especially where the firm is a partnership run along traditional law firm lines, with a strong hierarchy and the year-on-year growth of profit per partner is the overriding aim. The owners work within the business and are embedded in the small teams that form the essential framework of the Agile firm. They are often used to calling the shots, or at the very least having the final say on almost every decision. There is a big adjustment to be made for them to get comfortable with a flattened out, collaborative structure. Partners need to learn to take their ownership hat off at the door or, perhaps as much of a challenge, embody and then infuse their non-owner colleagues with the very best kind of owner mentality – a drive to deliver the very best service and collectively grow and develop the firm.

Compensation structures can be an obstacle in their own right. Especially for those working in firms with eat-what-you-kill, origination credits and the widest span of remuneration levels, who may find that underlying financial inequities and the imposed objectives required to maintain them, keep disrupting efforts to work along more bottom-up, democratic lines. Both partners and central management and support functions will probably feel a frisson of cold fear that pushing decisions and the ability to act quickly on hires, investments and change down to the team level is a retrograde step, risking taking the firm 'back' to the days of being a loose collection of cottage industries run on different lines based on the personal preference or whim of the local partner.

There is a lot of wisdom available to law firms who are serious about jumping these high fences. On the question of overcoming the inherent hierarchy and excessive deference to and control vested in partners, I think Josh Kubicki, who was at the heart of US firm Seyfarth Shaw's pioneering Agile journey, has some great advice. He has written an entire, short ebook on instilling *intrapreneurship* in law firms and his first suggestion is on the money:

> *Intrapreneurship is about allowing intrapreneurs to emerge from within the organization, not deliberately building certain people into intrapreneurs. It values ideas and collaboration from anyone inside the firm without regard for rank, title or pay.*[93]

Although using your early adopters, champions and advocates, especially within the partnership ranks, to sell and spread the message about the benefits of Agile is an essential element of the transition process, you will need to be wary about grand claims and over-promising. What Kubicki wrote about this in 2017 really captures one of the pitfalls for innovators and intrapreneurs in law firms. He advises:

> *just doing it and sharing it after execution. The wise intrapreneur understands that publicity triggers the firm's antibodies and immune system. Grandiosity inside a law firm breeds fear.*[94]

Moving a traditional law firm environment to a highly Agile model will never be easy or universally applauded along the way. You will be setting out to achieve a transformation in the face of inevitable, irrational but entirely understandable and predictable resistance. To do this it is imperative you create, or maintain, a high-trust environment, sometimes from a low-trust start point. That will involve buttressing your case with facts, demonstrating success from small pilots and building a cadre of enthusiasts and advocates from across the firm.

Which brings me neatly, and finally, back to clients. Clients are your not-so-secret weapons and the catalysts to success on your Agile journey. Ultimately, clients pull the strings in your firm, provided they are given a voice and you are prepared to invest time, effort and some money to dig deep into their needs. No Agile transformation is going to succeed without the engagement of the client voice.

Agile first steps – united by a common purpose
- Identify the purpose and 'northstar' that will enable you to keep your entire firm and Agile teams aligned and inspired. If you have already done this (which many will have) review it critically in light of this chapter and sources like *Start with Why* – does it make the grade?
- Communicate and keep repeating your simple purpose and ensuring it is in everyone's mind when they work and especially as they serve clients.
- Remember – start small, test and iterate. Identify your 'edge' and start scaling your Agile campaign there. Be patient about reaching the ultimate destination but get started right now.

Notes

1 Derek Southall, "The Rise of the MicroNed", www.hyperscalegroup.com/articles/2021/1/11/the-rise-of-the-microned.
2 See www.ana.net/content/show/id/pr-2020-word-year; 'agility' was the runner-up!
3 S Denning, *The Age of Agile: How Smart Companies Are Transforming the Way Work Gets Done*, Amaryllis, 2018, p17.
4 J Furlong, *Law is a Buyer's Market: Building a Client-First Law Firm*, Law21 Press, 2017.
5 G Beaton and I Kaschner, *Remaking Law Firms: Why and How*, ABA, 2015.
6 J Newton, *The Client-Centered Law Firm: How to Succeed in an Experience Driven World*, Blue Check Publishing, 2020.
7 HK Gardner, *Smart Collaboration: How Professionals and their Firms Succeed by Breaking Down Silos*, Harvard Business Review Press, 2017.
8 Michele DeStefano and Guenther Dobrauz-Saldapenna (eds), *New suits: Appetite for Disruption in the Legal World*, 2019.
9 R Susskind, *The End of Lawyers?: Rethinking the Nature of Legal Services*, OUP, 2008.
10 R Susskind and D Susskind, *The Future of the Professions: How Technology Will Transform the Work of Legal Experts*, OUP, 2015.
11 D Susskind, *A World Without Work: Technology, Automation and How We Should Respond*, Penguin Books, 2020.
12 Gary Hamel quoted in www.stevedenning.com/site/Default.aspx.
13 P Drucker, quoted in "These 10 Peter Drucker quotes may change your world", www.nbcnews.com/business/business-news/these-10-peter-drucker-quotes-may-change-your-world-wbna56060818.
14 www.agilealliance.org/agile101/the-agile-manifesto-2/.
15 *Id*.
16 *Id*.
17 JP Womack, DT Jones and D Roos, *The Machine That Changed the World*, Harper Perennial, 1990.
18 M Poppendieck and T Poppendieck, *Lean Software Development: An Agile Toolkit*, Addison-Wesley Professional, 2003.
19 Agile Lawyer, https://agilawyer.com/en/.
20 E Ries, *The Lean Startup: How Constant Innovation Creates Radically Successful Businesses*, Portfolio Penguin, 2011.
21 IDEO, www.ideo.com/eu.
22 Wouter Aghina *et al*, "The five trademarks of agile organizations", 2018, www.mckinsey.com/business-functions/organization/our-insights/the-five-trademarks-of-Agile-organizations.
23 Olli Salo, "How to create an Agile organization", 2017, www.mckinsey.com/business-functions/organization/our-insights/how-to-create-an-Agile-organization.
24 Darrell K Rigby, Jeff Sutherland and Hirotaka Takeuchi, "Embracing Agile: How to master the process that's transforming management", https://hbr.org/2016/05/embracing-agile.
25 Darrell K Rigby, Jeff Sutherland and Andy Noble, "Agile at Scale", https://hbr.org/2018/05/agile-at-scale.
26 S Denning, "How management is being transformed: Drucker Forum insights", www.forbes.com/sites/stevedenning/2019/11/26/how-management-is-being-transformed-drucker-forum-insights/.
27 *Id*.
28 S Denning, *The Age of Agile: How Smart Companies Are Transforming the Way Work Gets Done*, Amaryllis, 2018, p125.
29 J Furlong, *Law is a Buyer's Market: Building a Client-First Law Firm*, 2017, Law21 Press, p181.
30 E Ries, *The Lean Startup: How Constant Innovation Creates Radically Successful Businesses*, Portfolio Penguin, 2011, p72.
31 S Denning, *The Age of Agile: How Smart Companies Are Transforming the Way Work Gets Done*, Amaryllis, 2018, p123.
32 *Ibid*, p75.
33 J Furlong, *Law is a Buyer's Market: Building a Client-First Law Firm*, Law21 Press, 2017, p6.
34 *Ibid*, p5.
35 J Newton, *The Client-Centered Law Firm: How to Succeed in an Experience-Driven World*, Blue Check Publishing, 2020.
36 *Id*.
37 CLOC, https://cloc.org/.
38 Association of Corporate Counsel (ACC), www.acc.com/.
39 Antony Smith, "Survey Report: Key Challenges Facing Legal Project Managers", www.linkedin.com/pulse/survey-report-key-challenges-facing-legal-project-managers-smith/.
40 International Institute of Legal Project Management, "The IILPM LPM Framework", www.iilpm.com/the-iilpm-lpm-framework/.
41 CLOC, "Legal Project Management (LPM) for Legal Teams", https://cloc.org/wp-content/uploads/2019/03/CLOC-LPM-for-Legal-Teams-Feb2019.pdf.
42 PH Woldow and DB Richardson, *Legal Project Management in One Hour for Lawyers*, American Bar Association, 2014.

43 SB Levy, *Legal Project Management: Control Costs, Meet Schedules, Manage Risks and Maintain Sanity*, DayPack Books, 2009, p197.
44 Antony Smith, "Survey Report: Key Challenges Facing Legal Project Managers", www.linkedin.com/pulse/survey-report-key-challenges-facing-legal-project-managers-smith/
45 *Id*.
46 Solicitors Regulation Authority, "Statement of Solicitor Competence", www.sra.org.uk/solicitors/resources/cpd/competence-statement/.
47 John E Grant, quoted in Lena Boiser, *The Agile Law Firm: Achieving Success Using Kanban*, https://kanbanzone.com/2020/agile-law-firm-achieving-success-using-kanban/.
48 IDEO, "Brainstorming", www.ideou.com/pages/brainstorming.
49 J Kubicki, *Six Suggestions for Legal Intrapreneurs*, 2017, p15, https://joshkubicki.com/intrapreneur.
50 M Hagan, "Law By Design", 2017, https://www.lawbydesign.co/.
51 Vanderbilt Law School, "Legal Problem Solving", https://law.vanderbilt.edu/courses/395.
52 J Furlong, *Law is a Buyer's Market: Building a Client-First Law Firm*, Law21 Press, 2017, p136.
53 Legal Lean Sigma Institute, http://legalleansigma.com/.
54 ML George, *Lean Six Sigma for Service: How to Use Lean Speed and Six Sigma Quality to Improve Services and Transactions*, McGraw-Hill Education, 2003.
55 LawFirm Pricing, https://lawfirmpricing.com/about/.
56 S Denning, *The Age of Agile: How Smart Companies Are Transforming the Way Work Gets Done*, Amaryllis, 2018, p11.
57 *Ibid*, p20.
58 www.agilealliance.org/agile101/the-agile-manifesto-2/.
59 Lucy Adams, *HR Disrupted: It's Time for Something Different*, Practical Inspiration Publishing, 2017.
60 *Ibid*, p26.
61 *Ibid*, p58.
62 NetApps, "Netapp did it again! 13 consecutive years on the fortune 100 best companies to work for list", https://blog.netapp.com/blogs/netapp-did-it-again-13-consecutive-years-on-the-fortune-100-best-companies-to-work-for-list/.
63 Dave Cook, BigHand, speaking at the Legal COO Network virtual event *Lawyer Productivity*, chaired by the author, 21 January 2021, www2.bighand.com/coo_network.
64 *The Motley Fool*, "3 'monster' growth stocks I'd buy for 2021 and beyond", www.fool.co.uk/investing/2020/12/26/3-monster-growth-stocks-id-buy-for-2021-and-beyond/.
65 Richard Susskind quoted in *Legal Cheek*, "2020s is the decade of legal change, says Richard Susskind", www.legalcheek.com/2019/05/the-2020s-is-the-decade-of-legal-change-says-richard-susskind/.
66 Steve Sumner, "Creating the Agile law firm of the future", Legal IT Professionals website, www.legalitprofessionals.com/legal-it-columns/65-guest-columns/12237-creating-the-agile-law-firm-of-the-future.
67 Williams Lea and Sandpiper COVID 19 survey, https://info.williamslea.com/new-survey-reveals-shifts-in-emphasis-from-profits-to-people.
68 *The Economist*, 10 September 2020, www.economist.com/leaders/2020/09/12/is-the-office-finished.
69 BigHand and Association of Legal Administrators (ALA), The Legal Support Retirement and Staffing Survey, www.bighand.com/en-us/legal-retirement-and-staffing-survey/.
70 Reynen Court, https://reynencourt.com/.
71 Thomson Reuters, https://innovation.thomsonreuters.com/content/dam/openweb/documents/pdf/uki-legal-solutions/brochures/panoramic-customer-brochure.pdf.
72 Shakespeare Martineau, www.shma.co.uk/our-thoughts/shakespeare-martineau-announces-house-of-brands-strategy/.
73 S Denning, *The Age of Agile: How Smart Companies Are Transforming the Way Work Gets Done*, Amaryllis, 2018, p8.
74 PWC, *The future of industries: Bringing down the walls*, p3, www.pwc.com/gx/en/industries/industrial-manufacturing/publications/the-future-of-industries.html.
75 E Ries, *The Lean Startup: How Constant Innovation Creates Radically Successful Businesses*, Penguin, 2011.
76 *Ibid*, p77.
77 ANA, "'Pivot' Voted ANA 2020 Marketing Word Of The Year", www.ana.net/content/show/id/pr-2020-word-year – 'Agility' was the runner-up!
78 See C Christensen, *The Innovator's Dilemma: When New Technologies Cause Great Firms to Fail*, Harvard Business School Press, 1997.
79 George Beaton and Imme Kaschner, *Remaking Law Firms: why and how*, American Bar Association, 2016, p11.
80 Williams Lea and Sandpiper COVID-19 survey, https://info.williamslea.com/new-survey-reveals-shifts-in-emphasis-from-profits-to-people.
81 I Parker, *Successful Digital Transformation in Law Firms: A Question of Culture*, Globe Law and Business, 2021 (in press); quote taken from www.globelawandbusiness.com/books/successful-digital-transformation-in-law-firms-a-question-of-culture.

82 Sarah Blair, Thorntons Law, speaking at The Virtual Legal Tech Forum, October 2020 (Birmingham Law Society/Oosha).
83 Twilio, "COVID-19 Digital Engagement Report", www.twilio.com/covid-19-digital-engagement-report.
84 Peter Owen, Lights-On Consulting, speaking at The Virtual Legal Tech Forum, October 2020 (Birmingham Law Society/Oosha).
85 D Susskind, *A World Without Work: Technology, Automation and How We Should Respond*, Penguin, 2020.
86 J Furlong, *Law is a Buyer's Market: Building a Client-First Law Firm*, Law21 Press, 2017, pp69–81.
87 S Sinek, "How great leaders inspire action", TEDX talk, www.ted.com/talks/simon_sinek_how_great_leaders_inspire_action?referrer=playlist-the_10_most_popular_tedx_talks.
88 S Sinek, *Start With Why: How Great Leaders Inspire Everyone To Take Action*, Penguin, 2011.
89 John Hagel website, www.johnhagel.com/about/.
90 S Denning, *The Age of Agile: How Smart Companies Are Transforming the Way Work Gets Done*, Amaryllis, 2018, p125.
91 See C Christensen, *The Innovator's Dilemma: When New Technologies Cause Great Firms to Fail*, Harvard Business School Press, 1997.
92 See www.forbes.com/sites/stevedenning/2017/01/02/john-hagels-wake-up-call-for-business-how-to-launch-a-change-movement/?sh=478e9ebe63f6.
93 J Kubicki, *Six Suggestions for Legal Intrapreneurs*, 2017, p5, https://joshkubicki.com/intrapreneur.
94 *Ibid*, p6.

About the author

Chris Bull
Principal, Edge International
chris@edge-international.com

Chris Bull is a management consultant, retained adviser, business thinker and speaker focused on transforming the legal services sector. Throughout his career he has been one of the leading pioneers of alternative business models and transformation in the sector. His roles include COO and Chief Executive at mould-breaking law firm Osborne Clarke and COO for Europe & the Americas at alternative legal service provider Integreon. Chris has worked at all four of the Big 4 accounting firms and has advised on a series of high-profile alternative business structure launches in the UK for clients including KPMG and LegalZoom. Back in the early 2000s he was introducing open-plan agile offices, central transformation teams, process redesign practices and shared service centres into the law firm model, years before most UK or US law firms considered them.

His legal consulting career began in 2011 and he has advised, often in a retained role, multiple law firms and professional service organisations in the UK, North America and Asia as part of Edge International's strategy consulting team.

Chris has become one of the busiest speakers and chairs at legal business and innovation events. He is a judge for many legal sector awards, including British Legal Technology Awards and Modern Law Awards. He chairs the Legal COO Network and co-chairs the Bristol+BathLegalTech collaborative organisation, helping to steer what a 2021 independent report cited as a leading global legal tech cluster. His previous publications include *The Legal Process Improvement Toolkit* and *Law Firms in the Digital Age*.

About Globe Law and Business

Globe Law and Business was established in 2005. From the very beginning, we set out to create law books which are sufficiently high level to be of real use to the experienced professional, yet still accessible and easy to navigate. Most of our authors are drawn from Magic Circle and other top commercial firms, both in the UK and internationally.

Our titles are carefully produced, with the utmost attention paid to editorial, design and production processes. We hope this results in high-quality publications that are easy to read, and a pleasure to own. Our titles are also available as ebooks, which are compatible with most desktop, laptop and tablet devices. In 2018 we expanded our portfolio to include journals and Special Reports, available both digitally and in hard copy format, and produced to the same high standards as our books.

We'd very much like to hear from you with your thoughts and ideas for improving what we offer. Please do feel free to email me at sian@globelawandbusiness.com with your views.

Sian O'Neill
Managing director
Globe Law and Business
www.globelawandbusiness.com

New Special Report in law firm management

Globe Law and Business

Legal Practice Transformation Post-COVID-19

Jonathan Fortnam
Stuart Weinstein

Law firm management Insights

Legal Practice Transformation Post-COVID-19 imagines the post-COVID-19 world for legal services and asks what has changed, what will stay the same and what values are critical to ensure the successful operation of legal teams. This Special Report is aimed at lawyers in private practice, in-house counsel, professional support staff and all those involved in the delivery of legal services, to help them understand what the future of the profession will look like and, most importantly, how to thrive in it.

For full details, go to **www.globelawandbusiness.com/LPTP**